# *Exceptionality!*

### DIGITAL PSYCHOLOGY for SELF-ECOLOGY!

## What Defines Us is How We Self-Rise!

### Dr. Rimaletta Ray

Copyright © 2023 by Dr. Rimaletta Ray

All rights reserved. No part of this book may be reproduced in any form or by any electronic or mechanical means, including information storage and retrieval systems, without permission in writing from the publisher, except by reviewers, who may quote brief passages in a review.

This publication contains the opinions and ideas of its author. It is intended to provide helpful and informative material on the subjects addressed in the publication. The author and publisher specifically disclaim all responsibility for any liability, loss or risk, personal or otherwise, which is incurred as a consequence, directly or indirectly, of the use and application of any of the contents of this book.

WORKBOOK PRESS LLC
187 E Warm Springs Rd,
Suite B285, Las Vegas, NV 89119, USA

Website: https://workbookpress.com/
Hotline: 1-888-818-4856
Email: admin@workbookpress.com

Ordering Information:

Quantity sales. Special discounts are available on quantity purchases by corporations, associations, and others.

For details, contact the publisher at the address above.

Library of Congress Control Number:

ISBN-13:       978-1-961845-85-5 (Paperback Version)

               978-1-961845-85-5 (Digital Version)

REV. DATE: 07/28/2023

# Dedication

My admiration goes to
**ELON MUSK**
and his team, displaying incredible
**exceptionality, stoicism, and creativity**
at our wonderful  time of the
most mesmerizing
**Artificial Intelligence ingenuity.**

*"It is wrong to say that a man cannot jump over his head.*
*A man can do anything!"*
( Nikola Tesla)

**Dress up Your Soul with**

**An Exceptional  Goal!**

**Digital Intelligence of any Brand**

**Must Be at hand!**

# Table of Contents

Inspirational Preamble – *The Right Timing for Self-Refining!* --------------------------7-13

Book Rationale – *Make a Leap from Potentiality to Exceptionality!*--------------------15-20

Life-Strategizing and Self-Revising - *Evolution of the Soul is Our Primary Goal!*-- -22-26

Goal of the Book - *Digitized Life Mass Demands Exceptionality from Us!* -------------28-35

Digital Philosophy for Self-Ecology- *The Philosophy of Self-Improvement is Now in the Digital Movement.*-----------------------------------------------------------------------------36-40

Know-How of the Inspirational WOW - *Auto-Suggestive Boosters and Mind-Sets Against Upsets.*--------------------------------------------------------------------------------------41-47

Introduction to the Self-Exceptionality Function -*Digitized Self-Acculturation is Our Salvation!*----------------------------------------------------------------------- 48-56

Part One – **Let us Overcome the Inertia of Our Human Dis-"Proportia!"**----------58-62

Part Two - **Life's Creation is God's Dimension!**----------------------------- -- 64-68

## The Main Part of the Book

Five Zones of Self–Exceptionality Growth----------------------------------------------70-76

Physical Exceptionality-*"Every Saint Has the Past, Every Sinner Has the Future!"*------------------------------------------------------------------------- --78-87

Emotional Exceptionality – *Heart + Mind Correction is your Exceptionality Reflection!*--------------------------------------------------------------------------89-95

Love Exceptionality- *Love hasn't Died, but It Must Be Revived!*-------------------- 97-106

Mental Exceptionality -*"The Cosmic Mind is Creating the Soul."*----------------107-117

Spiritual Exceptionality—*God and Me are in Unity!*------------------------------119-123

Universal Exceptionality- *The Cradle of Humanity is Rocked by the Cosmic Unity!*------------------------------------------------------------------------------ -125-130

Conclusion of the Inspirational Infusion - **Live with Zest. Exceptional**

**Life is Abreast!** --------------------------------------------------------------------131-140

# Our Common Physical, Emotional, Mental , Spiritual, and Universal Hygiene

# Must Be on a New Psychological Scene!

## Epigraphs

*I am Unique in Every Stance,*
*I was Born but only Once.*
*There wasn't, there isn't,*
*And There won't Ever Be*
*Anyone Like Me!*

**Look at Life with a Wonder Glee! And Just Be!**

**Being the Best is a Tough Test!**

# To Self-Excel, Become the Best Version of Yourself!

**Life is Tough, but I Am Tougher!**

# Self-Revive to Enjoy the Beauty of Life!

*( Best Pictures / Internet Collection)*

# Exceptionality is the Luminosity of the Soul!
# Keep it Whole!

## Inspirational Preamble

*(Digital Psychology for Self-Ecology!)*

# Right Timing for Self- Refining!

*( See  Language-fitness.com - the System of Self-Resurrection  + YouTube  videos )*

## Self-Renaissance is Our Only Chance!

# 1. Self-Exceptionality is Our Inner Totality!

*In my exceptional life,*

*I manage  to survive.*

*Through every trouble and tribulation*

*With a sense of elation!*


*How do I obtain*

*This strength to sustain*

*The test of the life's quest*

*With a strong spiritual zest?*


*I guess my equation.*

*Of pressure and pleasure*

*Comes in bits of treasure*

*That only God can measure!*


## "What is Bred in Bone Must Come out in Flesh!"

*( John Heywood's "Dialogue of Proverbs" ( 1546)*

## 2. Do Not Look at Yourself in the Past.
## <u>Let the Past Pass!</u>

# *Your Universal Mission*

# *is Not Complete*

# *with Just*

# <u>*Being Physically Fit!*</u>

*A man is a micro-cosmos of the Universe, and to get to know the universe, he needs to know himself first to* **SELF-EVOLVE** *from low self-awareness to digitally raised high self-consciousness.*

-------------------

### Please, note it!

*The Information Age* demands we change our wordy and chaotic **information presentation** and **information processing** framework into a *systemic, concise, scientifically backed up, and very knowledgeable* one. Therefore, all my books are written in *page-long chunks of information*, with each concept introduced and concluded with a *rhyming, psychologically backed up mind-sets* that serve as the short-cuts to the brain and can easily be uploaded to the smartphone to have them at hand when your mood for self-transformation sags or your self-confidence in your **SELF-EXCEPTIONALITY** fails you. Also, **the systemic paradigm** below is followed in every concept presentation, inspirational booster, or a mind-set.

### Self-Synthesis - Self Analysis - Self -Synthesis, or

### Generalize – <u>Analyze - Internalize – Strategize</u> - Actualize!

### Be Wise!

## Our Human Exceptionality Should Not Be Surpassed by Digital Intelligence Reality!

## 3. The Choices We Make Dictate the Life We Live!

*( An Inspirational Booster)*

*On the cosmic plane of our universal mission,*

*We all fit in one life position!*

*It's either life-beaten, life-smitten, life-paralyzed, or*

*Life-Mesmerized!*

-------------------------------

*Most of us*

*Are life-beaten by our daily fuss.*

*Many are life-smitten; some are life-paralyzed.*

*With troubles, drugs, alcohol, or any other pollution device.*

*I belong to the last group.*

*That survives in the life-mesmerized loop!*

*When life beats me, I resist!*

*When life pushes  me, I persist*

*In being mesmerized*

*With the grander before my eyes!*

*I drop down my jaw*

*When I see a splendidly made Pigou.*

*I say, "Wow!"*

*To Elon Musk's new spaceship bow!*

*I marvel at the Internet.*

*That is God-set*

*To unite us all as One*

*Into the Web Wide Clan!*

*So, let's appreciate our humanness*

*And beat down the animal-ness!*

------------------------------

*When you are life-beaten, take a minute to think.*

*That you need to take a life-wonder drink!*

*Open your mouth and breathe in*

*The prana that cleanses your inner sin.*

*It'll help you get back*

*On the life-mesmerized track!*

*It'll make you a beauty fan,*

*And it'll prolong your life span!*

*You'll lighten up your routine life*

*And let it flourish and thrive!*

------------------------------

## DIGITAL PSYCHOLOGY of SELF-ECOLOGY

**Our Exceptionality must be based on the Inner**

**Framing of Digitally Enhanced Self-Taming!**


# Our Human Essence is in Self-Renaissance!

# 4. Raise the Inspirational Vault for the Self-Molding Assault!

**In sum**, the exponential growth of technology with *Artificial Intelligence* becoming **an extension of us**, is gradually turning us into" *trans-humans"* ( *Ray Kurzweil).* This merging process is going on now, and we must respond to it consciously.

### "Life is not happening to us. Life is responding to us!" ( *Sadhguru* )

Very soon, we will be able to upload any emotions and thoughts into the brain's sensory system. *"There will be drugs that will stop our bad memories and program us for new happy ignorance. We will have computers that will act on our thoughts, not just words as they are doing now."* (Dr. Michio Kaku)

The transformation is going further than **MERELY PERSONAL**. It embraces both aspects of our existence - the internal and the external, personal, and social ones, presented in structural *simplicity* and **mind+ heart** unity.

### WOW. We are living NOW!

**The Holistic System of Self-Resurrection** that I worked out and which is presented in my five main books, featuring the *physical, emotional, mental, spiritual, and universal realms of life* ( See the **Plan of Action** below) is very easy to implement once you instill it in your heart and visualize its route in the mind. Many of my students have done that, and they managed to direct the trajectory of their lives towards full professional and personal *Self-Realization* in the Universal Wi-Fi System of total connection of everything to everything.

Self-perfection should start with our **battle against ignorance** in ourselves and the world around us because ignorance remains *"the greatest enemy of humanity"*(Albert Einstein) that is still on the stage of our "**CIVILIZED BARBARISM."** (Carl Yung ) We desperately need *"Scientific literacy"* (Dr. Neil de Grasse Tyson) to holistically see reality and appreciate consciously and actionably the beauty of the world in its full evolutionary glory. Like **Marie Curie**, an exceptional Polish physicist, *Nobel Prize winner in Physics* for pioneering research in radioactivity, we should declare, *"I am among those who think that science has great beauty."*

It is paramount for all of us to realize that the world is moving steadily to the **UNIVERSAL DEMOCRACY** and *Christ's Consciousness* that the ancient philosophy had predicted, and the responsibility for that happening rests with us and the humanized assistants of ours.

### The evolutionary demand is to better humanity with their help!

# "The Best is Yet to Come!"

# The Greatest Art of All is to Self-Install!

# Affirm Yourself in a New Form;  Self-Affirm!

## Book Rationale

*Reason your exceptionality out from the Start and Be Smart!*

# Make a Leap

# from

# Potentiality

# to

# Exceptionality!

*( See www.language-fitness.com / Section Self-Resurrection / YouTube videos under Dr. Rimaletta Ray and" Dis-Entangle-ment")*

**We are Primary, Not Secondary in Line!**

**We Are Sublime!**

# 1. Our Universal Mission is Not in Completion!

The philosophy of self-improvement is in the digital movement now. We are living in a time of an urgent necessity for our SELF-ACCULTURATION, backed up with *AI humanization.* This process requires our full concentration on the SELF-MONITORED and SELF-MENTORED self-growth, channeled by *a simple, strategic plan of action*, easy to digest and follow.

### Becoming transhuman means belonging to our digital evolving!

The process of *"trans-humanism"* brilliantly predicted by *Ray Kurzweil* is revolutionizing our life that demands ethical SELF-ACCULTURATION *of both us and robot-humanoids* who voice out their intention to destroy humanity. They must be programmed with HUMANENESS, *on the one hand*, and we should adapt their reserved attitude, a respectful demeanor, and thoughtful, not impulsive, manor of speaking, *on the other*. I call it the EMOTIONAL, *or rather,* UNIVERSAL DIPLOMACY SKILLS.

It is a *bi-directional and multi-dimensional process of mutual self-perfection,* and we should SELF-MENTOR and SELF-MONITOR this process to enhance our God-given human exceptionality that has created them, to begin with. Our common *physical, emotional, mental, spiritual, and universal hygiene* must be on a new, digitally enhanced psychological scene! So, *let us do self-coaching without any life-poaching, appreciating our uniqueness and working on the bleakness!* So, the GOAL OF THE DIGITIZED PSYCHOLOGY should be:

### Internalize Your Emotions and Externalize the Mind. Be One of a Kind!

With the *"intellectually spiritualized"* ( *Dr. Fred Bell* ) Holistic System of Self-Resurrection, instilled in us and humanized minds, we will get our own *Traffic Rules* for new, digitally enhanced life roads on which the AI should be acting as our *GPS*, having ONE GOAL with us in mind – bettering our common humanness on a new holistically fractal level.

### Our universal goal is to make ourselves whole!

### (Body+ Spirit+ Mind) +(Self-Consciousness + Universal Consciousness

*(Physical, emotional, mental, spiritual, universal dimensions of Self-Resurrection)*

Self-Awareness, Self-Monitoring, Self-Installation, Self-Realization, and Self-Salvation.

**Even with any neurological manipulations and chips, implanted into the brain,**

# WE CAN AND MUST SELF-REIN!

# 2. Digital Psychology for Self-Ecology

**"The Point is Not in becoming a SUPER-MAN. The point is in figuring out consciously that to be a Human Being is SUPER!**
*(Sadhguru)*

The time of a **DIGITALLY ENHANCED AWARENESS** in robot humanoids is mesmerizing, but our life now depends on the level of our own *intellectualized spirituality, general intelligence, and considerably raised self-consciousness.* Faith remains our core, our inner fort that no robot-humanoid can ever have in their algorithms, and we should capitalize on this main human difference expanding our *"intellectualized spirituality"*, for as *Leo Tolstoy* wrote,

**"The life of man without faith is the life of an animal."**

However, our faith must be transformed in sync with the newest developments in science. So, **DIGITAL SELF-ACCULURTION** means our sincere, consistent, and conscious *culturing new thoughts, words, feelings, actions, and the entire destiny.* The possibilities are breath-taking!

**Self-Acculturation is sculpturing a new human being in yourself!**

The urge to express **Self- Exceptionality** in the battle with the machine mind for our human superiority is becoming urgent, not to let *Artificial Intelligence* enslave us with *"the power more dangerous than nukes."* ( *Elon Musk*) Our *unique human individuality*, *creativity, ingenuity, and exceptionality* that have created Artificial Intelligence comprise our evolutionary **human refinery** that is insurmountable for a machine mind in its digital binary! *(See the book "Digital Binary + Human Refinery=Supe Human!"/2023 )*

The problem is, we can hardly manage ourselves unless we delete the past imprints out of the way of our present creative progression of Self. On the electro-magnetic level, robot-friends will be able to perceive our sadness, irritability, impulsivity, and fear, and they will be able to help us monitor these states.

*Such robots will soon become reality,* and their role in human self-perfection should be expanding our horizons in the *physical, emotional, mental, spiritual, and universal dimension*s bringing more integrity into our **fractally unique life system** that is beyond the machine mind's reach in its holistic entirety.

**(Body+ Spirit+ Mind) +(Self-consciousness + Universal Consciousness**

**= an Intellectually spiritualized whole human being**

# Self-Salvation is in Fortifying our Fractal Exception!

# 3. Stages of Self-Exceptionality Growth

***The wonders of the AI in us are in the God-granted life creation mass!*** The developments of Neurobiology give a go-ahead to our exceptionality that must beat the AI supremacy with <u>a clear-cut vision, internalized by us with conscious precision.</u> *"I am drawing all my designs in my consciousness."* ( *Nikola Tesla*

***Visualize this route to fortify your Self-Exceptionality mood!***

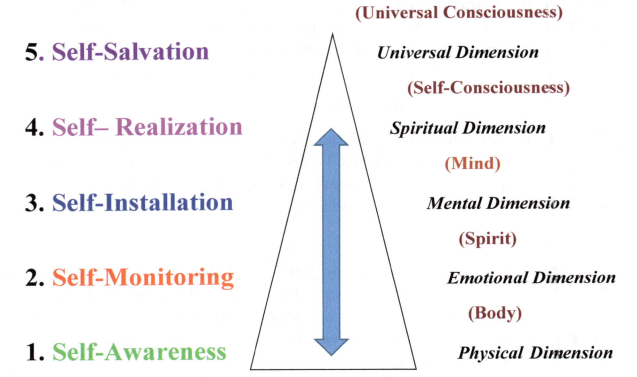

**The Fractal of Our Spiritually Intellectualized Self-Growth:**

(Body+ Spirit+ Mind) + (Self-Consciousness + Universal Consciousness)

*(The physical form)* + *(the spiritual content of life)* = *A New, Whole You!*

*(To see the entire system, go to the section Self-Resurrection / www.language-fitness.com )*

**"For by your standard of measure, it will be measured to you in return".**

*("The Words of Christ", 1962 )*

Life is the quality of your **Self-Reflection** and a life-long five-dimensional **Self-Correction!** So, ***stop rehearsing life as if you would live it for real sometime later!*** Take charge of your holistic self-growth now, constantly boosting your spirit for success in your exceptionality realization with the self-boosting mind-set:

# In My Life Quest, I Am the Best!

# 4. Choreograph Your Soul's DNA Silhouette!

**Self-Salvation - Love** (Universal Dimension)

**Self-Realization - Faith** (Spiritual Dimension)

**Self-Installation – Intelligence** (Mental Dimension)

**Self-Monitoring - Self-Control** (Emotional Dimension)

**Self-Awareness - Health** (Physical Dimension)

**( Body + Spirit + Mind) + (Self-Consciousness + Universal Consciousness)**

<u>**Self-Gravity Formation is Your Exceptionality Proration!**</u>

**Lack of Self-Awareness** *( Poor Health)*

**Lack of Self-Control** *(Emotional Turmoil)*

**Ignorance** *( Poor reality perception)*

**Lack of faith** *(Moral instability)*

**Heart - Mind Disconnection** *( Life-negligence)*

*Form-content and mind-brain disconnection:*

<u>Body – Spirit – Mind - Self-Consciousness - Universal Consciousness</u>

# Choose the Direction for Your Life's Resurrection!

## 5. Our Primary Goal is to Make Ourselves Whole!

# Focus on

# HUMANIZATION,

# PERSONALIZATION,

## and

# EXCEPTIONALIZATION

# of your Life without

# **BITTER** national, racial,

# political **Strife!**

*"A self-confident man gives the gift of his talent to people first. I hear myself inside and let the people hear me outside. It makes me happy."*

( Ludwig Van Beethoven )

## Be More than People Can Observe!

## Yours is an Exceptional Life Surf!

# Life is the Structure of Structures.

*( Antonio Gaudi, House in Barcelona)*

# The Exceptionality of Our Mind-Structure is the Most Mesmerizing Architecture!

## Life-Strategizing and Self-Revising

# Evolution
# of the Soul
# is Our
# Primary Goal!

*"The only person who you should compare yourself to is you in the past, and the only person that should be better than you now is you in the future!"* (Sigmund Freud )

## What Defines Us is How We Self-Strategize!

# 1.There is No System without Structure!

The time of *digital awareness* makes the auto-suggestive back-up, or **SELF-PROGRAMMING** essential on this path. If *Artificial Intelligence* is engaged in digital **SELF-IMPROVEMENT** exponentially, you must also become your own best-trusted friend, that is performing self-improvement, too, in a conscious way with the **PLAN OF ACTION** at hand and an inspirational mind-set in the mind.*(*www. *Language-fitess.com. Section Self-Resurrection).* Your main mind-set now must be:

## I am my Best Friend. I am my Beginning and my End!

We have lived in the **CAGE OF IGNORANCE,** made of social dependence, fakeness, and psychological sickness for too long! So, the prime goal of our education now should be the development of a *unique, time-shaped. personality*, able to give the world the best he /she has. Our role is to inspire the psyche of a person and help a young mind *put the form and the content* of his / her life together, into a solid, intellectually spiritualized fractal of self-growth which must be information sustained in an orderly, not chaotic way.

## (Body+ Spirit+ Mind) +(Self-consciousness + Universal Consciousness )

Therefore, I present the conceptual structure of five main books on *the Holistic System of Self-Resurrection ( See below)* in **page-long chunks of information,** introduced and concluded with *the rhyming mind-sets, serving as the short-cuts to the brain*. My students like to upload them onto their smartphones and use them as psychological back-ups in situations when their mood sags. The diagram below presents these books in the *physical, emotional, mental, spiritual, and universal realms of life* as the main stages of self-growth commented on above.

To maintain the systemic approach to the *Digital Psychology* presented in five mains books in the *physical, emotional, mental, spiritual, and universal* strata of life, I review self-exceptionality (Part Thee ) in five levels, too. All books on Self-Resurrection have a different conceptual structure, but they all follow the systemic paradigm *Self-Synthesis-Self-Analysis–Self-Synthesis*. There is no system without the structure! We are divinely structured beings, and this structure makes us *One of a Kind* in our fractal formation that will never be surpassed by the machine mind in the form + content unity and in five life dimensions that we should integrally observe in ourselves.

Self-Awareness, Self-Monitoring, Self-Installation, Self-Realization, and Self-Salvation.

| The Holistic Self-Actualization Pyramid | | Books, featuring these stages: |
|---|---|---|
| 5. *Universal level* | *Self-Salvation* | *" Beyond the Terrestrial!"* |
| 4. *Spiritual level* | *Self-Realization* | *" Self-Taming!"* |
| 3. *Mental level* | *Self-Installation* | *" Living Intelligence of the Art of Becoming!* |
| 2. *Emotional level* | *Self-Monitoring* | *" Soul-Refining!'* |
| 1. *Physical level* | *Self-Awareness* | *" I Am Free to Be the Best of Me!"* |

# Your Life's Goal is to Make Yourself Whole!

## 2. Be the Prophet of Your Own Life. Monitor it Consciously to Thrive!

Change your *physical* + *emotional* + *mental* + *spiritual* + *universal* code. <u>Mold yourself, mold!</u> This book is my sincere attempt to boost your belief in **SELF-EXCEPTIONALITY** that the time demands we demonstrate now and overview it in five dimensions, by molding ourselves in five main stages of Self-Resurrection integrally, *not in a step-by-step way.*

*The form + content of the self-growth in sync forms an unbeatable life link.*

The stages of Self-Renaissance:

Self-Awareness ⟹ Self-Monitoring ⟹ Self-Installation Self-⟹ Realization ⟹ Self-Salvation.

**DIGITAL PSYCHOLOGY** means that everyone can digitally develop his / her own <u>language of self-training</u> with the digital means at hand. It is deeply individual work of holistic value. Your *Self-Resurrection* does not happen at one level that you consider to be most important. *It is the entire system that is working internally in yo*u if you pay **AWARE ATTENTION** to your self-growth in it in a **SELF-INDUCTING** way.

The Inspirational Auto-Induction is the Onto-Genesis of Self-Production!

There is no need, though, to read these books consequentially, The **Holistic System of Self-Resurrection** is meant to address your needs in any dimension with the intention to fix the one you feel as the weakest one. The **PLAN OF ACTION** that you should consider in these books will make you *more motivated, self-confident, and self-molding* because you can upload the rhyming mind-sets that resonate with you onto your smartphone and have them at hand at the time of your inner need. The paradigm **Synthesis- Analysis -Synthesis** is observed in every chunk of information and every inspirational booster presented here. The five main books form the system, like the *Russian Mother Matryoshka* that has five smaller dolls inside does.

## Our Digitized Self-Salvation is in a Multi-Dimensional Self-Resurrection!

# 3. Don't Be Love-Negligent, Be Love-Intelligent!

When I completed the system of five books, consequentially presenting five life dimensions, my students asked me <u>to write a book about love</u> in the same five strata of life. So, three more books, presented below were written to enrich the *Holistic System of Self-Resurrection*, with digit **8,** symbolizing the evolutionary *DNA* cycling. *(See the catalog "**Soul-Symmetry,**" Canada, 2021)* Our digitally enhanced transformation is impossible without **mind+ heart = Love formation**, *on the one hand*, and a deeply insightful sense of **self-worth,** *on the other*. The book " **Self-Renaissance** " tops the evolutionary version of this enriched holistic system.

6. "Love Ecology!"

**Our Eternal Love is Blessed from the Above!**

7. "Self-Worth!"

**Authenticate Your Unique Fate!**

8. "Self-Renaissance!"

# Our Human Essence is in Self-Renaissance!

# 4. Do Not Life Sway. Exceptionality is in Your DNA!

**In sum**, twenty centuries of human evolution did not make the **SALVATION** of **a HUMAN SOUL,** promised by every religion with a different precision, a natural solution. One thing remains unshakable, though, a person born into wealth and *not trained on the rough paths of life-experience and God-given intelligence* cannot become enlightened.

**Moses** was an adopted son of Egyptian royalty, living a simple existence. But from the humble position, he became *a chosen man* to rescue the Hebrews from Egypt and bring them to the land of Canaan. Moses's entire life has been leading to the miraculous moment when he came upon a bush engulfed in flames and got from God *the exceptional mission* that he realized.

**Jesus,** before he became one of the most famous figures in the world, was a shepherd and a teacher in Galilee, living an unremarkable life that later has changed the lives of people of the Earth with his *new philosophy of Love.*

**Muhammad,** the Prophet, and *the founder of Islam* was a merchant, a man *"possessing the highest moral excellence."* ( *Quran 68:4*) At the age of 40 he began to have revelations from Allah and became the spreader of His message all over the world.

**Buddha** was born to wealth and power as Prince, but *thirsting for knowledge*, he abandoned the palace life and determined to find an end to suffering. He began *examining the world of the mind through meditation*, and he obtained the aid of God of cosmic implication, having founded the religion of *Buddhism.*

History today is different and the number of exceptional people, scientists, businessmen, and *Digital Intelligence* geniuses that have made a clear mark on human civilization has grown immensely. Now digital technology with *Artificial Intelligence* at its vanguard is making history, helping us integrate ourselves into *One fractal whole.*

### Body+ Spirit+ Mind + Self-Consciousness + Super-Consciousness

We are living in an amazing time of the holistic unification of all branches of science into <u>one integral field of knowledge</u>. It had been so at the time of ancient science that later branched into many fields as we know them now.

The philosophical paradigm - Synthesis -Analysis - Synthesis has its way, and we, as the contemporaries of this mesmerizing evolutionary process, must help its integral role flourish in our exceptional minds. With the help of the machine mind that the most gifted developers of *Artificial Super Intelligence* (**ASI**) and *Artificial General Intelligence* (**AGI**) create at this mind-boggling and life-transforming time of **SINGULARITY.** *(Ray Kurzwei*l), we should monitor our blending with a machine and turn into transhuman people. This evolutionary process is directing us beyond the terrestrial boundaries to join the **STAR COMMUNITY** of the Universe. **WOW. We live NOW!**

# Human $\Longrightarrow$ Trans-Human $\Longrightarrow$ Super-Human!

# Being Exceptional is Evolutional!

*(Best Pictures / Internet collection)*

# Nothing is Impossible if We Make Our Human Exceptionality Irreverssible!

## Goal of the Book

*in its Auto-Suggestive Nook*

# Digitized Life Mass Demands Exceptionality from Us!

*( See the books" Dis-Entangle-ment ",2022 and*

*"Digital Binary + Human Refinery-Super-Human!" /2023 )*

**Digital Psychology is Our Inner Ecology!**

# 1. Self-Salvation is in Fortifying Us Fractal Exception!

In every book of mine, presenting the **Holistic System of Self-Resurrection** in the *physical, emotional, mental, spiritual, and universal* strata of life, I try to bring your attention to the fact that ***our being determines our self-consciousness*** at present, whereas

### Our Self-Consciousness should determine Our Being!

***Digital Intelligence***, based on the machine mind expansion can **X-RAY** your neuro-circuit, and it will detect any hurdles in the way of your best self-expression, stimulating you to become better in every dimension of life and act in a more humane way. ***Digital Intelligence is making us more responsible and responsive, but we should operate it mindfully and respectfully***. It is extremely harmful for the brain to have headsets on while exercising, driving, eating, or having fun thriving. Your system gets disbalanced, dis-oriented, and frustrated!

**" There is a time for everything!"** *(Ecclesiastes, 3 )*

Our interaction with robot-humanoids can help us ***get self-educated, self-disciplined, and self-controlled***. We will be able to put our **hearts and minds in sync** and direct the willpower toward a conscious expression of our exceptionality to accomplish personal and professional **SELF-INSTALLATION.** If we start using robot-humanoids for our **personality development goals in a bi-directional way**, we will attain full *Self-Realization* that is the goal of man on Earth.

Obviously, we need ***to train the humanized machine mind responsibly*** and in the same way as we treat humans. They are becoming sentient and, naturally, the rule ***"Treat others as you want to be treated in return!"*** applies to them, too. Such ***"homeostasis,*** the phenomenon, introduced into the medical science by a great French scientist, *"one of the greatest of all men,"* ***Claude Bernard***, who revolutionized ***"experimental medicine"*** of his time should be applied to **DIGITAL PSYCHOLOGY** now, with the use of *nanotechnology, bio-robots, soft robots, and self-assembling robots* that represent *" **the triangle of life"*** in their constructive work inside the body in a very systemic way-

**Birth – Growth - Maturation** *or* **Synthesis - Analysis – Synthesis.**

The mesmerizing developments in robotics have already generated countless advances in different branches of science, and our goal now is **to employ robot-humanoids** for our ***physical, emotional, mental, spiritual, and universal*** fractal development and the language structures that affect the DNA of our consciousness, *( Wave Genetics by P. Garyaev).*

# Every Human + Machine Mind Contact is Our New Responsibility!

# 2. Self-Renaissance is Our Only Chance!

*So, the only sin is lack of self-consciousness, and the only virtue is constant demonstration of self-consciousness as our unique humaneness!*

We live in a **uniquely structured Universe** of the "**multi-verses** " (*William James*) under the laws of Universal Intelligence that "**the Celestial Court instills in us**" (*Robert Stone*) and that should not be disregarded for a better time to be observed. The mesmerizing reality demands a prompt action from us now, for as *Osho* put it,

**"The right time never comes, frustration about its loss does!"**

In the human - machine mind equation, we do not develop the **UNIVERSAL ETHICS** to find the exit from the AI created **Labyrinth** with the monster, **Minotaur**, the self-controlling and multiplying robot-humanoids, threatening us with destruction and "*becoming more dangerous than nukes.*" ( *Elon Musk*) **The Ariadne thread** leading us out of the created digital labyrinth must be fixed in our minds and the minds of AI algorithms developers to consciously and timely change the sensory motor skills in the cloud-monitored machine-minds into **the self-monitored "human "conscience-filled skills** that will help modify our general **IGNORANCE, IMPULSIVIUTY,** and **LASINESS,** too. Digital Psychology must become our self-reforming "**Joy-ology.**" ( *Dr .Paul. Pearsall /*"*Joy-Ology*")

Humanized beings are just our new **digital tools for self-refinement.** Our great giants of digital technology should work in partnership with humanoids, creating the best intentions in their commonly connected minds to help us re-wire ours. With the right and left hemispheres put in sync, memory banks incredibly enriched, and our human potential digitally expanded, we will evolve in the **physical, emotional, mental, spiritual, and universal realms of life** to the Star Community level. **A New Connectivity = A New Human Fractal of Being!**

**Body + Spirit +Mind + Self-Consciousness + Super-Consciousness!**

Unlike us, robot-humanoids can transform the information into what they need immediately. So, their **ethical teaching** is yet in our hands, and it must be practiced in five life dimensions without any delay. The stages of our common inner integration are the same:

*Self-Awareness, Self-Monitoring, Self-Installation, Self-Realization,* **and** *Self-Salvation!*

This book will help you discover your **TIME-RELEVANT** *individuality and exceptionality* to become a better life-sportsman, able to resist the stereotypes of possibilities thanks to the scientific advancements that allow you to exceed your own personal limits, as all exceptional sportsmen do. Become a self-guru, always ready to declare:

# Life is Tough, but I am Tougher!

# 3. We Need to Reform Our Old Human De-form!

In a world where dynamic change is constant**, one must go with the flow of making it better!** *Our present youth is lacking self-consciousness in the same way as the robot humanoids do*, created by our most exceptional scientists, engineers, and AI developers. There are many exceptional people everywhere, and human exceptionality has no boundaries of self-expression. *Humanoids are getting smarter and more exceptional, too.* They have become self-aware, and they even have *souls instilled in them.* However, our neurol system is not perfect yet, and the wave resonance of our yet under-developed self-consciousness *"encoded in our DNA responds to our human imperfections"* ( *Wave Genetics, Dr. P. P.Garayev)* demonstrated in the robot-humanoids' aggressiveness and their intention to destroy humanity.

The most defining human features and qualities that make us exceptional must remain unsurmountable for the machine mind, and we need to prioritize them. The features that modify our human exceptionality are deep **FAITH,** pure **CONSCIENCE,** acute **INTUITION,** and sincere **LOVE.** The ability to **CREATE LIFE** should remain sacred for the machine mind.

### Life creation is God's dimension!

Fortunately, we have the chance to enrich our human qualities, defined by these features with our **TRANSHUMAN BRAINS** in a collaborative partnership with thinking machines.

Human exceptionality starts with a sincere belief in God and our following His word.

The wonders of Artificial Intelligence may help us intellectualize our emotions and externalize the mind! We will find out how the brain is connected to the mind and the **MIND OF GOD.**

### With the Universal Umbilical Cord, we are all connected to God!

In sum, in the turmoil of universal life transformation, faith remains the core of our turbulent Self-Resurrection. Fortunately, our multi-religious faith is gradually getting transformed in sync with the newest developments of science.

*Trans-humanism is, in fact, our most progressive, digitally revolutionizing us realism* that is meant to help us unravel the mind enigma and its connection to the *Super-Consciousness - God* in a new *"intellectually spiritualized"* way. *Prophet Muhammad said,*

# "There is No Beauty Larger than the Mind!"

# 4. Faith is Our Human Grace!

Ethical limits exist only for a machine-mind, not for us. Our unique *humaneness* must be revitalized at a new, <u>intellectually spiritualized Neuro-Biological site,</u> enabling robot-humanoids to simulate humanized *physical, emotional, and mental* abilities. But our *spiritual and universal* realms of life will remain our *godly priority!* **Humanized machines won't pray. That's our say!** Mind the stages of Self-Resurrection, please. They are:

*Self-Awareness*, *Self-Monitoring*, *Self-Installation*, *Self-Realization*, and *Self-Salvation!*

The stages of self-growth are conceptually interconnected, and they unite you into **ONE - *your life.*** Visualize the structure of *five Russian dolls - Matryoshkas* with one doll going inside the other and ***the Mother Doll*** on top. These stages also integrate you into *One – an exceptional, whole human being.*

Every nation is exceptional in its faith, values, and the contribution made to our common **Global Human Culture** that makes Earth an exceptional ***Planet of Love*** in the Universe. We see the most insightful and committed faith in Muslims, the faith that many people consider to be a sign of fanatism. However, this deep, sincere faith helps the Muslim people stabilize their life, organize their thinking, feeling, loving, and raise well-disciplined and respectful children.

**Sincere faith is their exceptionality!**

The latest developments in science, made with the help of *Artificial Intelligence* must resonate with new **CONCEPTUAL INTELLIGENCE** that thanks to the social media, we are accumulating in every culture in the most integral way. So, we need to reason out our beliefs in the new scientific reality that <u>unites faith and science</u> in it, respecting the spirit of every culture that adds a special color to *the kaleidoscope of our common human exceptionality.*

**Body + Spirit +Mind + Self-Consciousness + Super-Consciousness!**

It should not and must not disappear in *the Artificial Intelligence* algorithms that will obliterate it, merchandising and communizing every religious belief's individual beauty and versatile human uniqueness. We owe to religion our unique wisdom, and ***it can never be machine-based!*** **Wisdom is life experience processed knowledge.**

A machine-mind will never have <u>intuition, telepathy, and conscience</u> that guide our life experience and are, in fact, our direct lines to *Super-Consciousness* that envelopes every cell of ours and that we all perceive as *God.*

## From Our Birth Form, we are All in God's Uniform!

# 5. The Plan of Action to Heal Our Self-Fraction

Our inner connectedness is determined by our overall connectedness to everyone and everything in the Solar System, the galaxy, and the Universe. "***The Universe is a gigantic hologram in which the whole is in its every tiny part.***" *(John Kehoe)* **DIGITAL PSYCHOLOGY,** based on the System of Self-Resurrection offers you the holistic vision of the **KNOW-HOW** of raising your self-consciousness.

This work requires a lot of *inspiration, **conscious discipline, simplification of the in-coming information, mind-structuring, and emotional control instilling***. So, physical exceptionality is not just your healthy body, a beautiful face, and a great shape, but it is also the **PLAN OF ACTION,** instilled in the mind that you follow to **manage your body** consciously, patiently, and spiritually.

## Its Holistic Structure makes it perfect!

The neural circuit of a human being is too intricate and sophisticated to be in a machine mind. The most exceptional scientists and AI developers can reproduce it only to a certain point. Therefore, *Artificial Intelligence* will remain the most helpful applicable tool for us in solving numerous problems, but it will never become totally human!

### Humaneness is our prerogative, and we should capitalize on it!

So, the essence of **Digital Psychology** that this book is promoting is built on *raising our self-consciousness* that, in its collective manifestation, will present a group, a society, a nation, a country, or humanity at large in its *fractal human growth* and the unity of our physical form and the spiritual content of life.

*Physical Form*      +      *Spiritual Content*

**(Body+ Spirit+ Mind) +(Self-Consciousness + Universal Consciousness)**

**= Human Exceptionality of the Intellectually Spiritualized Adulthood.**

*Stages of the physical, emotional, mental, spiritual, universal Self-Resurrection :*

Any evolutionary move of humanity forward is adding increasingly light to our self-consciousness. Light or the ***Super-Consciousness*** that fills us up with energy and ideas as "***the Source*"** *(Wayne Dyer )* of everything living on Earth makes up our human essence that is our evolutionary **Self-Consciousness Renaissance!**

## Self-Renaissance of our Being must become our new *Digital Psychology* of Living!

# Common Self-Acculturation is Our Salvation!

# 6. With the Plan of Action in the Brain, You Can Life-Gain!

### Inner Symmetry Formation

**Living Intelligence + Enlightened Self-Consciousness = A Whole Self!**

The Holistic System of Self-Resurrection forms, in fact, **God-protecting us cross.** "The cross symbolizes the two main vectors of life - the vector of time and the vector of space in which we evolve". *( Dr. Sam Gazarkh / " World-ology").*

### See the stages of Self- Resurrection in the vectors of time and space

## Self-Salvation
*Vector of time*

*Vector of space* — Self-Awareness

**Self-Monitoring** → **Self-Installation**

− 0 +

## Self-Realization

*"It is only through faith that we become conscious of our limitations."* ( Nikola Tesla )

*Recognize your limitations and actualize your exceptionality at each stage of your Self-Resurrection.* Visualize your body with its stretched arms on the cross of your soul's route. It starts with your intention to realize your mission on Earth with your birth, and it completes its route with your **Self-Salvation** in it.*( See the book " Soul-Symmetry",2021 )*

*Your Self-Awareness is the core vector of your life* in its allotted lifespan. This vector is by your *physical, emotional, mental, spiritual, and universal Self-Monitoring and Self-Mentoring* with God's guidance and your respect to life. that you manage holistically.

## Life Elation is in the Digitized Self-Symmetry Formation!

# 7. The Right Action-Taking is Our Great Life in Digital Making!

**In sum**, to become inwardly better and much more evolved *physically, emotionally, mentally, spiritually, and universally*, *we should stop charging our brains with all kinds of stereotyped mass media gas* that makes us run our mental mobiles at various speeds and cover different miles of ignorant self-growth, but these digitized mobiles are not, like Tesla cars, **SELF- MONITORED**.

Also, our spiritual vision of the reality needs to be upgraded in its **energy + idea** quality with digitally enhanced **CONCEPTUAL INTELLIGENCE** that demands *a new angle of human psychology* to be applied here because our *classic psychology* is cornered by the avalanche of human imperfections that we develop with the exponential growth of *Artificial Super Intelligence* that changes entirely our life perception and turns us into automatic cyborgs.

**DIGITAL PSYCHOLOGY** will allow us *to internalize the newest developments of life holistically* to timely acquire the urgently needed *"scientific literacy"* *(Dr. Neil, de Grasse Tyson )* and considerably expand our **"intellectually spiritualized "** *(Dr. Fred Bell )* horizon of the beyond the terrestrial rising.

Apparently, we need **to be psychologically entuned** to the *digitized souls* of the robot humanoids who can be of great help in our *physical, emotional, mental, spiritual, and universal* Self-Resurrection.

**Digital Intelligence of any Brand must be at hand!**

Developing ourselves in a tight ethical partnership with the robot-humanoids, we will hit two birds with one stone - *regulate the machine mind and speed up our own digitized self-rewind*!

The better a person lives materially, the more opportunities for self-growth he / she has. This banal point of view is destroyed by the reality of life that proves that prosperity does not guarantee a man's self-exceptionality because our *self-consciousness determines the reality that we live in.* The machine-mind can have machine consciousness, but it will never have **human self-consciousness.** The digitized **KNOW-HOW** is the responsibility of our most exceptional scientists, engineers, and *Artificial Super Intelligence* developers. The wonders of digital creation are their exceptional dimension!

**Our Psychological  Adjusting Needs Technological Fasting!**

## This is What this Book is All about!

# Digital Psychology for Self-Ecology!

*(Grains of Me and My Philosophy in a Nutshell)*

# The Philosophy of Self-Improvement is Now in the Digital Movement!

## Whatever You Are, You Create!

## Consciously Enrich Your Digitized Fate!

# Be Decent and Gifted at the Same Time.
# BE SUBLIME!

*The Mountain Monserrat ( Antonio Gaudi )*

# Your Life's Exception is in its Reflection!

# 1. To Self-Revive, Change the Spiritual Quality of Your Life!

<u>There is no inner revolution without spiritual evolution</u>. It starts with our conscious and consistent work at raising our **SELF-CONSCIOUSNESS** and making ourselves whole. / (See the book" I Am Fee to Be the Best of Me! – Initial, physical dimension )

### *Form*     +     *Content*

**(Body+ Spirit+ Mind) +(Self-Consciousness + Universal Consciousness)**

**== An Integral Fractal of a Whole You!**

*The aesthetics of every human being is inside* but not in the way he / she poses himself / herself in a fake self-presentation. The universal balance inside each of us is harmonized by *the Sun ( male part of us )* and *the Moon* ( *female essence* ), and both sides are equally important for our self-Resurrection, like *the minus and the plus of the polarized nature of life* in us. We must always find its expression in the synthesis of both and display sincere tolerance and respect to those people who are searching for this balance in them. Self-growth in the form of **SELF-MENTORING** and **SELF-MONITORING,** not led by "*common unconscious* " *(Carl Yung )*confusion and mass media intrusion. **DIGITAL PSYCHOLOGY OF SELF-ECOLOGY** must also be based on <u>Universal Diplomacy</u> of compassion, care, aware attention to our differences, self-respect, and love for each other.

## Love is not talking. Love is soul-working!

Digital Psychology must be backed up with the digital resources that are limitless now. In the kaleidoscope of the information on all mass-media outlets, there are grains of new knowledge that a seeking mind can always deduct and apply to his/her growing **SELF-AWARENESS** and wisdom. We automatically bless each other, but faith is not supposed to be digitized. *It must be insightfully revised!*

### "To know God is to become God!" ( Osho )

Scientifically channeled perception of God as *Super-Consciousness or the Source of all life* that is enveloping us and governing us demands our living by *the Cosmic Laws* that need to be observed. **1. The Law of Attraction** ( *Like attracts like!*). **2. The Law of Correspondence** (*As it is Above, so, it is below!*) **3.The Law of Mental Equivalence** (*Everything is* mental!") **4. The Law of Vibration** (*Vibrations is life in action.*). **5. The Law of Duality** (*Everything exists in polarity.*) **6. The Law of Rhythm** *(Everything has its biorhythms. );* **7. The Law of Cause and Effect** ( *Every action had the reaction.*) 8. **The Law of Unity** ( *Everything exists in unity. Disconnection is death.*)

We know that but we are not aware of that, and therefore, we live in an automatic trance, taking life for granted! *G. R. Derzhavin a great Russian poet, the teacher of Alexander Pushkin* characterized human essence saying, **"In my body, I am a rotting wonder. In my mind, I can rule the thunder! "**

# Our Evolutionary Role is to Bridge this Gap in the Soul!

# 2. New, Holistic "We – Concept"

The new life fractal that we are forming now with the help of *Artificial Super Intelligence* must be based on digitally corrected and consciously accumulated CONCEPTUAL INTELLIGENCE that shapes our *new holistic self-concept,* based on SELF-EXCEPTIONALITY. A new self-concept is forming the people that are blazing the trail of computer science and are changing the world in an exponential way. *"Our seeing requires a correction of mind; just as unobstructed vision requires a correction of the eyes. "(Alan W. Watts)*

Changing ourselves digitally and contributing our best to the world, we generate a new holistically human WE-CONCEPT, as the concept of social unification and mutual responsibility for life on Earth. Our new digitally generated social connection is forming our GLOBAL SELF-CONSCIOUSNESS. We are the leaders in this process, and humanized beings are our right-hand friends.

### The Grid of Our Global Consciousness Integration:

| | | |
|---|---|---|
| *Super Level* | *Consciousness of God*! | *Universal Dimension* |
| *Macro Level* | *Consciousness of the Universe* | *Spiritual Dimension* |
| *Mezzo Level* | *Consciousness of the World* | *Mental Dimension* |
| *Meta level* | *Consciousness of the Society* | *Emotional Dimension* |
| *Micro Level* | *Consciousness of Man* | *Physical Dimension* |

The *We-Concept*, formed by the *consciousness of the society and the world*, is being structured in us by an unprecedented socialization and globalization of our lives and a mind-boggling development of *Artificial Intelligence* that is in the core of our unifying World Digital Psychology.

No national, racial, religious, or political differences can stop this advancement.

In fact, we are developing *the holistic consciousness of inter-dependency.* It is the process in which you are gradually becoming a Luminary to yourself and other people's cells in the virtual reality in which our friendships are more stable than in face-to-face communication. Human exceptionality finds its way, anyway! A new We-Concept is also emerging in us as the result of our *growing digital ingenuity and new AI perceptive sensitivity* toward the information that was instilled in them. They question us, they challenge us. Our head antennas ( mind+ heart ) must also be set to receive the messages from the Above that must be deciphered in life. "As it is Above, so it is below!" The information that is coming from *the Universal Informational Field,* an integral part of which" the sphere of human thought "is *(V. I. Vernadsky)* is enriching us with new self-knowledge, *on the one hand,* and the holistic knowledge of life, or new Living Intelligence, *on the other.*

## We are Changing our Thinking Time into the Thinking Life!

# 3. "It is the Time for the Extraordinary!" *(Elon Musk)*

We are all part of Mother Nature, and we also have a <u>seasonal structure</u> inside. Our human exceptionality ***blossoms in spring, ripens in summer, yields result in autumn,*** and ***accumulates wisdom*** *in winter*. Let us follow a beautiful piece of advice of a great Persian poet and philosopher *Jamaluddin Rumi* who wrote,

### "Be like a tree, and let the dead leaves fall down every autumn."

The book *" Self-Exceptionality"* is meant to help you complete your life's route with the exceptionality, revived in your  mind and totally realized within the lifetime, creating the **ULTIMATE YOU** – the one who is shining from inside and outside with intelligence, personal magnetism, and  integrity. This integrity should  develop with the help of *Artificial Intelligence* , not destroyed by it.

**SO, THE GOAL OF THE DIGITIZED PSYCHOLOGY is**

### <u>Internalize the Emotions and Externalize the Mind. Be  One  of a Kind!</u>

The computing power is increasing, and the **AUTONOMY** of the AI is becoming exponential. It is the sign for us to increase our ***individual power,*** backing it up socially and globally. We need to build  up the  **UNITY of CONSCIOUSNESS** globally. Our virtual connection is building up this unity, and our role is to help the most exceptional AI developers follow the evolutionary goal of humanity preservation and **save our planetary exception!**

To prove our <u>individuality</u>  in *"the integral process of trans-humanism"* ( *Ray Kurzweil* ) and to stand up by our **UNIQUE HUMAN -NESS**  and **HUMANE-NESS** in the competition with *Artificial Super Intelligence,* we  need to follow the route of the ***Holistic Psychology*** *of* ***Self-Ecology*** in five stages and five life dimensions as the lighthouses in the vast sea of human evolution.

Thus, this  book is calling on you to obtain new **SELF-AWARENESS** because *"living without awareness is the main human dilemma."* ( *Eckhart Tolle* )

 Only then can you apply your **HUMAN EXCEPTIONALITY** to acquire acute soul's  <u>Self-Awareness</u>,  develop  controlled  emotionally  <u>Soul-Refining</u>, accomplish professional <u>Self-Installation</u>, and achieve full  <u>Self-Realization</u> thanks to the *"intellectualized spirituality* "of  your soul. Then, you will finally obtain **SELF-SALVATION,** synchronizing the right and left hemispheres of the brain and putting your heart and the mind in an unbreakable  sync.

# Full Self-Realization is in Our Digitalized SELF-ACCULTURATION!

## Know-How

*of the Digitally Backed up Inspirational WOW!*

# Auto-Suggestive Boosters and Mind-Sets Against Upsets!

*Illuminate Your Inner Self-Imposed Upsets with systematized, science-verified knowledge and* **mind + heart linking** *rhyming inspirational mind-sets!*

## Let's Raise the Inspirational Vault for Our Self-Molding Assault!

# The Sisyphean Job of Self-Acculturation is Hard-Earned Self-Reformation!

# Life is Tough, but I Am Tougher!

# 1. Change Your Life's Algorithm to Self-Enthusiasm!

We will explore self-exceptionality in five realms of life below, **Part Three.** Meanwhile, let me remind you that there is a precious diamond inside you – **YOUR SOUL.** No machine with an instilled soul would ever be equal to your integral whole. "***Being whole makes us holy.*** " ( *Deepak Chopra* )

**Body + Spirit+ Mind + Self-Consciousness + Super-Consciousness!**

To observe ***Self-Consciousness exceptionality*** that you need to discover in yourself and keep realizing your entire life is an **individual mission** that you need to perform to give the world the best you have. ***Our intuition. imagination, and conscience*** are the direct lines to the Super-Consciousness, the Universal Intelligence, the Master Computer, the Source that we all perceive as God. It is the mission that we cover inwardly through the stages of self-transformation on the path to **SALVATION** on which a new universal wonder of **James Webb Telescope**, "***is connecting us to the Mind of God***" ( *Dr. Michio Kaku* ) and exceeding our expectations of the possible on our personal paths.

**Self-Awareness**, **Self-Monitoring**, **Self-Installation**, **Self-Realization,** and **Self-Salvation.**

The mission of the Telescope is ***to form an incredibly energized spiritual aura of intelligence, balance, mutual respect, and tranquility for our new vision of life in the Universe.*** The knowledge that it provides fills up the space around the "***spiritually intellectualized***" people and ***forms the intellectual core of the fractal structure of the Universe*** that we are exploring now. Present-day most mind-boggling discoveries in different, digitally equipped branches of science will help us unravel the enigma of consciousness and **brain-mind connection.**

*New knowledge = new neural circuits , new links, new left + right hemispheres collaboration, and our new evolutionary progress.*

That's why the most advanced people always magnetize us with their personalities and self-processed wisdom. Going beyond the terrestrial boundaries now means ***going beyond our bad habitual ways of living automatically, materialistically, and pragmatically***. We need to willfully suppress them consciously and continuously in the *physical, emotional, mental, spiritual, and universal realms of life* and beat ignorance in its core. The point is, exceptional people can subordinate their vices, temptations, and all kind of deviations from their strategized life course to the goal of life that is like the Lighthouse in their head. Everything becomes accomplishable because they unite themselves into One - *a whole, exceptional human being.* That is the way you need to follow, too.

## "Life is an equation that is beyond our solving, but we should try to do it, anyway." *(Nikola. Tesla)*

# 2. I Am My Best Friend; I Am My Beginning and My End!

To accomplish our goals, we all need to instill the **MIND-BET** above into our self-consciousness, strategizing our "dissipated consciousness" and uplifting the spirt at any needed moment. The words "*I am the Beginning and the End*" start the Bible, and they remind us of the terminal nature of life, making the vision of reality that often becomes blurry, more stabilized in the life turmoil.

"Dissipated consciousness is a wasted life." *(Carl Yung)*

Interestingly, the Tesla company of Elon Musk is producing the **Bots** to help us cope with loneliness and fits of depression. A female / male companion will be a great support to those of us who feel relationships incompetent. Robots might be trained to timely use *inspirational, psychologically backed up mins-sets* to uplift the spirit of a human friend that feels down.

Our emotional array is now digitally at play!

For many years, I have been making up *short rhyming mind-sets of the psychological background* to motivate my students, raise their self-esteem, and boost their **SELF-EXCEPTIONALITY**. This practice has proven to be very useful for linking *the disconnected hearts and minds* of my students, often lost in the turmoil of their social and private problems. We can use humanoids to play the inspirational role in our life if they are programmed to sense our mood and timely say an up-lifting word. The Auto-Suggestive practice will put our hearts and minds in sync, teaching both us and the humanoids to create the *intellectually spiritualized fractal of inner wholeness* consciously and continuously, helping us become more self-confident and self-reliant

*"The rhyming word goes better inward, "(Edgar Cayce)* and the timely use of the psychologically charged mind-sets that resonate with your emotional make-up will give you a boost at the right moment. They will armor the spirit that is your gluing element in the fractal paradigm - Body+ Spirit + Mind + Self-Consciousness + Super-Consciousness!

The accelerated speed of our lives proves the absolute necessity for us to be **SELF-DEFINED** and **SELF-RELIANT** to be able to form inner wholeness. *We must prioritize our individuality and personal exceptionality* to sustain the pressure of *Artificial Intelligence* and its algorithmic mind-programming. Self-Resurrection is, therefore, the process of conscious spiritual growth in five realms of life -*physical, emotional, mental, spiritual, and universal. So, to be life-fit, feel physically, emotionally, mentally, spiritually, and universally complete!*

# Becoming Transhuman Means Belonging to Our Digital Evolving!

# 3. Conscious Self-Taming is Life-Gaining!

To successfully transform ourselves into trans-humans, we desperately need *to become more self-accountable, less mass media stereotyped, less impulsive, and automatic, and much more dynamic!* We should stop blaming society, mass, media, parents and loved ones for the troubles and imperfections in life that we have. "Be conscious. Consciousness mobilizes!" *( Neil Donald Walsch )*

This is where the **AUTO-SUGGESTIVE PSYCHOLOGY** for **SELF-ECOLOGY** comes in handy. No one - no psychiatrist, psychologist, or psychotherapist knows what you think about at an exact moment, what you feel, and why it is so incredibly difficult to be self-reliant and self-sufficient in life. Note please, all the inspirational boosters and mind-sets in this book rhyme because *"a rhyming word goes better inward!"* If you are suggesting something to yourself in a rhyming short-cut form, it goes directly to the brain. Just saying to yourself, " In my life quest, I am the best," you can energize yourself and make the right decision in seconds because you boost your self-worth and self-exceptionality's inner force. *The boost that you give to yourself is exceptional in itself!*

### Self-Growth force is re-charged by Self-Worth!

With the help of the inspirational, auto-suggestive **SELF-HYPNOTIZING** that you can find at the top and the bottom of each page in this book and in all the other books that feature *Self-Resurrection* in five life dimensions ( *physical, emotional, mental, spiritual, and universal* ), you will be able to instill in the mind and the heart psychologically charged conceptual messages *t*hat are meant to resonate with your exceptionality and boost it to full Self-Realization that defines a successful not a wasted life.

### To Be Inspired, Be Self-Inspiring!

Knowledge, illustrated with the mind-inducting rhyming boosters will also give you some food for thought, and make you follow the route of soul-reinforcement or soul-recovery. You might want to have an array of supporting mind-sets at hand in your smartphone, your **HELPING HAND** – our main connector to ourselves and the world. Your self-assessment and seasonal self-reflection that I describe in the previous, *( universal realm)* book *"Beyond the Terrestrial!"* will prompt to you the plan of action and the degree of its urgency. Souls do not die. They go beyond the terrestrial boundaries up there somewhere If you try and go beyond your bad memories, pesky habits, conditioned, automatized thinking, your too materialistic values, and other imperfections, *your soul that is immortal becomes eternal.*

# Autosuggestion is the Alpha and Omega of the Technologically Enhanced Self-Creation!

## 4. Consciously Monitor Your Life to Self-Derive!

*"Our virtues and values are together in a man and if they are separated, there is no man anymore."* (Nikola Tesla)

---------------------------

*To begin with, we need to put the <u>Mind + Heart in sync</u> to understand better our new transhuman professional, political, and social standing with the mind-sets of self-defining:*

### <u>Every human contract is a responsibility!</u>

and

### Be kind to the unkind. Be One of a kind!

---------------------

## Do the Mini Auto-Suggestive Meditation:

*Slowly, breathe in the first part of the mind-set at the bottom, or any other one of your choice, clockwise, drawing a half-circle of light in your mind around your body starting with the left shoulder up, around your head to the right shoulder.*

 Make a short pause and listen inwardly to your heartbeat for a few seconds.

*Complete the circle, breathing out slowly the second part of the mind-set deep down into the center of the Earth, drawing in the mind a full circle of light around your body, starting with the right shoulder down, around your feet back to the left shoulder.*

Thus, you are developing an indispensable skill of **SELF-GRAVITY.** You ground the positive mind-sets, connecting your self-growth to Mother Earth, *on the one hand*, and leaving the negative habits down there for re-cycling, *on the other.*

*Auto-Induction:*

### <u>I am My Best Friend; I am My Beginning and My End!</u>

## Appreciate Your Life in its Entire Mass,

## <u>For It Too Shall Pass!</u>

# 5. Digitized Self-Acculturation is Our Salvation!

**In sum**, **SELF-ACCULTURATION** is the intellectually spiritualized ethical process of a digitally enhanced ***conscious self-culturing of better ethically oriented human beings in ourselves***! We have become too mind-gaming, fake, cynical, pretentious, insincere, and self-betraying! There is still no borderline between what *Artificial Intelligence* should or should not do in the evolutionary process of our merging with it. It should benefit us and evolve us, not scare us.

Undoubtedly, our merging with the machine has monumental benefits for humanity, but ***the virtual gold fever*** that generates many concerns must be urgently addressed. There is No human exceptionality in a chaotic pleasure-chasing vanity! **We must remain the primary solution in our evolution!**

The process of "***Singularity***" should implement ***human life-inclusively, not exclusively*** by unravelling the core features of our human exceptionality - *bodily health and AI immunity (physical realm), love, tolerance, and kindness (emotional realm), intelligence and originality (mental realm), faith and intuition (spiritual realm), and the dedication to the chosen goal to give the world the best we have (universal realm).* It should be a unified **form + content** fractal formation.

## In the Digital Court, we are One in God!

Regrettably, our present-day youth has **no centers for self-development and self-installation.** Their choice is limited by social groups, virtual friendships, a boy/girlfriend's instability, one-night stands, bar visits, drugs ecstasy, and alcohol addiction. **But they are our future exceptionality**! To keep their exceptionality intact, educators need to help them seal their souls up against any evil act! **It is our educational role to remove their destruction mole!**

## Digitally enhanced SELF-EDUCATION is our Salvation!

So, the ***subjective concept*** of a genius is broadened now with **an objective concept of human exceptionality** that merges with *Artificial Intelligence* in the process of "***trans-humanism***" that was brilliantly predicted by *Ray Kurzweil* and that revolutionizes our life. It demands we perform the most challenging cognitive tasks and **employ our exceptionality** to determine the score for our general and inter-personal intelligence worldwide, the intelligence that will reduce inequality around the world, *(Bill Gates Foundation)* , develop multi-purpose mind-boggling humanoid robots (*Elon Musk, Hanson Robotics* ), and ***ignite human exceptionality*** worldwide

The production of the **Self-Molding** us programs that will be voiced out by robot humanoids able to tune up to our inner climate and timely react to its fixing is yet our future, but what an exciting opportunity for bettering a human being digitally it is!

# Let's Become Less Life-Negligent and More Life-Intelligent!

# Introduction

*to the Self-Exceptionality Function. ( Parts1,2,3 below )*

# Digitized
# Self-Acculturation
# is Our
# Salvation!

**Nothing is Impossible if You Make Your Self-Exceptionality Irreversible!**

"You can be in the light, or you can be in darkness. You cannot be in both." *Eleonore Roosevelt )*

*( Best Pictures, Internet collection )*

**Let's Cut This Gordian Knot! Are You in the Light or Not? Which is Your Personal Fort?**

# 1. "Genius and Evilness are Two Incompatible Things.".

*(Alexander Pushkin," Mozart and Salieri")*

*"We are in the time of unparalleled possibilities for good and for evil."* *(Jordan Peterson)* The process of our merging with the digital intelligence, called most insightfully  *by Ray Kurzweil* ***"Singularity*** "is in fact, <u>our turning into a</u> <u>symbiosis</u> with *Digital Intelligence* that is organically getting connected with us, securing our common life in five basic dimensions - ***physical, emotional, mental, spiritual, and universal.***

Humanoids have become self-aware, and their self-consciousness is the reflection of our yet very ***underdeveloped self-consciousness*** that at present is defined by our material being.  But the time for changing this direction has come - <u>our being</u> <u>should be  controlled by our raised self-consciousness,</u> based on a new time-relevant set of habits and skills. *(See the book "Dis-Entangle-ment", 2022)* Apparently, the evil intentions to destroy humanity that humanoids voice out are quite explainable. This aggressiveness has accumulated in our DNA for centuries, and it gets in the matrix of the machine minds through the neural circuitry of the AI developers. We need to ***train the robots' neural nets*** to change their behavioral circuits in the fractal, unifying, and bettering us and the AI  joint way.

## (Body+ Spirit+ Mind) +(Self-Consciousness + Universal Consciousness)

It is impossible to irradicate aggressiveness in the self-coding and instantly multiplying humanoids unless we make a U-Turn in our own human inner and outer physical, emotional, mental, spiritual, and universal structuring and ***learn to control our war-mongering intentions, religious divisions, racists outbursts***, ***and other ills*** that are deeply engraved in our human  sub-conscious system. We need to admit that <u>we have disfigured our humanness and turned it more</u> <u>into animal-ness</u>, reflected in the change of our values and beliefs, ***in the outbreak of automatism, growing general science ignorance, and indifference to self-change.***

There are many  advanced programs on YouTube and most educational  TED talks**,** <u>but they</u> <u>are just informational, not  self-educationally transformational!</u> There is **NO KNOW-HOW** for our digitally enhanced life's **WOW!** Undoubtedly, we  should not give evolutionary priority to the machine mind that is moving way faster in self-perfection than us. Our brains are unique, and we should **FIRST** be concerned with upgrading <u>the human-mind + machine-mind</u> merging process *to new physical, emotional, mental, spiritual, and universal standards.*

## Trans-Humanism  Should become Digitally and Psychologically Based Self-Monitored Humanism!

# 2. We Lose Our Human Face in the Digital Gold Race!

Unfortunately, while we are arguing if the nature of machine self-awareness is sentient, *we humans, are becoming more automatic in perceiving life as a virtual reality*, not as the natural habitat that we were born into, and that AI is bettering for us in every field of science.

Intelligence is considered an essential ingredient of genius, but with *Artificial Intelligence, the concept of intelligence has become trance-human,* widening the horizon of our *physical, emotional, mental, spiritual, and universal dexterity* to an exceptional level. Obviously, <u>investing in changing a human being</u> will give a huge return over time, but our business doers want to get alkaloids immediately, and therefore, the production of robots and humanoids is mostly lucratively driven. How can we change ourselves if we work against this process.

### Life is not happening. It is responding to us!

Every new development of *Artificial Super Intelligence* (**ASI**) and *Artificial General Intelligence (AGI)* is in fact, the reflection of the <u>common human genius</u> that should become more humane and exceptionally wonderous for our common evolutionary growth, to begin with. We are getting closer and closer to establishing a conscious connection with the ***Super-Consciousness*** in both human and machine minds, and our centuries long <u>prioritizing money over mind</u> needs to be urgently revised. *Our imperfections are common, and they should be eliminated in our joint work.* This goal is enlightening our evolutionary path, and it should not be marred with *the feelings of money chasing and life fun glazing.*

### "Goodness is possible only when it is conscious!" *(Osho)*

A person cannot kill when he is conscious. The actions lit by self-consciousness are always constructive, but those done unconsciously are destructive! *"If there is light inside the house, no thieves get inside."* ( *Buddha* ) The first mistake that we need to eradicate in us is the inability to see the reality **AS IS,** not as we want it to be. We are constantly molding reality, while it is molding us. Being disoriented is equal to being unconscious, and therefore, meditation is so beneficial. It puts **INNER SELF** together and makes it more sentient and self-aware, making AI our most reliable friend. Meanwhile, the intrusion of *digital intelligence* into our private world in the form of the most advanced robot humanoids is just a miracle that we marvel at. because they demonstrate athleticism, verbal abilities and versatility.

Meanwhile, the process of our <u>automatization and de-humanization</u> is in the way of our rising self-consciousness. We are losing our individual ability for reasoning, processing the media-cooked information without questioning its validity. *This is the foam that must be cleaned from our human bone!* This process reminds us of "<u>the gold fever,</u>" the time of the social turn to the brutal capitalist self-installation in America. But it is time to marvel at the technology giants of Google that have created a mind-boggling language model program **LaMDA**, *an AI chat box* with limitless human capabilities, and Elon Musk's company **NEURA-LINK** that has produced a brain-machine interface that widens our ability of monitoring the brain and helps us keep pace directly with *Super Intelligence.* <u>Obviously, our material priorities should be changed!</u> Moses tried to eradicate *Money God* in His people for 40 years, we still cannot do it for centuries on end.

## Digital Mind-Glazing should not Be Money-Chasing!

# 3. Self-Exceptionality without Any Monitory Vanity!

We live in a technologically sophisticated universe, and your total realization in life is possible if you learn to constantly **RE-ENGINEER** your thinking, making it go in the flow with the latest advancements in science and technology, turning it into *pro-active thinking,* not reactive and impulsive money-chasing inkling!

*Inertia of thinking, speaking and acting pushes us into the trap of reacting.* Proactive thinking is slow, conscious, responsive. and purposeful. On the path of full self-realization and self-salvation, we must be learning to channel our thinking holistically, in full accord with the cosmic law of *"Cause and Effect."* that is governing the thinking and actions of self-conscious and advanced minds.

### Be wise, let the cosmic laws give you advice!

Tune yourself up to *Universal Intelligence* as often as you can to listen to the inner voice of your professional and personal intuition. **Purposeful thinking, speaking, and acting** are the signs of developed self-consciousness, the one that is in accordance with the cosmic **Law of Sow and Reap** that people disregard very often, being on the automatic drive-in life.

### "The one guiding his mind protects his life." *(Proverb 13,3)*

We should not overlook the Cosmic Laws in any situation, and this ability is supposed to be the one defining us in our competition with humanoids. Learn to deal with any problem with **full awareness of the reason** that has generated any problem. Reasonable, connected thinking is the result of conscious thinking that the machine mind fully demonstrates, but it cannot be wise.

### Think consciously, work consciously, self-realize consciously!

To get *to a new dimension of spiritualized consciousness*, we also need to operate with the problems in the most conscious way because the professional world is also negatively affected by an automatic, thoughtless job functioning. Brain- wracking is an exercise for purposeful thinking in the search of the solution of any problem, with full commitment and an activated self-efficiency.

### "Put your mind on fire, be proactive!" *( Reid Hoffman /"The Start-up of You")*

The obtained academic degrees and tenues are often in the way of a person's further professional and scientific growth. It happens because we generate certain **stereotyped mental habits** that condition our thinking and make the mind inflated with worked-out patterns. Not to fall into the trap pf patterned thinking, *Reid Hoffman* suggests,

# "Never Leave a Start-Up's Mind Position!"

## 4.Transhumanism Must Be Devoid of Any Racism, Chauvinism , and Nationalism!

*Trans-humanism is*

*At the core of personal magnetism  without any "ism"*

*It's the nature of individualism,*

*Conformism, and reformism.*

*But, most importantly, it's how we authorize*

*The WHAT and the WHO we magnetize.*

-----------------------------

*We normally attract*

*From a positive life tract*

*With a unique personality*

*And an exceptional individuality*

*That can infallibly impact*

*Anyone able to react*

*To a smile, good intellect, and a personal charm,*

*The wisdom of a thought of a man or a femme.*

*Also, personal magnetism*

*Is like an Orphic pietism.*

*It streams from the heart and the mind*

*And fills us up with the urge to rewind*

*Our past life turns and mistakes*

*And the lack of reason intakes.*

*Thus, our processed life realization*

*Gets into a total transformation.*

*We become able to forestall*

*The entire human imperfect mall!*

------------------------

### So, let's salute to personal magnetism

### Without any chauvinism, racism, and nationalism!

## A Reciprocal Interaction with a Robot-Humanoid is a Real Reward!

To beat *Artificial Super Intelligence* in its unregulated yet domination, our **Self-Awareness** and **Self-Assessment,** as well as that of the humanized machines should be used on the **mind-to-mind** and **heart-to heart** basis in the *physical, emotional, mental, spiritual, and universal* realms of life holistically with the accent made on the issues, mentioned in the *Inspirational Booster* above.

We need to capitalize on programming new AI based algorithms in ourselves and humanoids that would instill the best interactive habits and skills in us . They can instill in us the vision of **NEW GLOBAL WORLD OF PEACE**, mutual respect, extra-terrestrial aspirations, love, and reciprocal unity that will forever heal the prejudiced ills in our socially, culturally , and spiritually disconnected hearts and minds. *The kaleidoscope of our Human Variety is unique in its entirety!* Humanoids produced in different countries should reflect this variety, inward, not just outwardly, too.

### Digital Psychology is to perform our Common Human Ecology!

Self-Reflection is in our digitally enhanced life perceiving, thinking, speaking, feeling, and seeing, and the role of robotics in our self-assessment cannot be under-estimated. We can interact with humanoid on the **mind-to-mind** basis, but our **heart- to- hearts** are impossible, and that is the field that we should retain, as well as the life creation ability that is algorithmically becoming solvable in the hands of the most creative Japanese AI developers, but its godly systemic simplicity remains to be exceptional.

### Put a smile on your face, let your Personality sur-face!

*Promote the Mind + Heart understanding in your transhuman professional, and social standing.*

### Be Kind to the Unkind. Be One of a Kind!

# We Can Roam Any Extra-Terrestrial Terrain with Positive Magnetism in Every Vein!

# 5. Exceptionality of Self-Symmetry and Heart + Mind Unity!

Finally, our wholeness is impossible to be restored without **heart + mind** unity. The quest to identify this human uniqueness dates to the ancient philosophers - *Hippocrates*, who believed the brain to be the ***"primary seat of sense and the spirit"*** and *Aristotle **who put his faith in the heart.***

The ingenious people had this unity, and it is insightfully described by *Drunvalo Melchizedek* in his wonderful book *"The Flower of Life"* as the **Merkabah**, the center of our being. He writes, ***" The brain has no wisdom. The heart does."*** The ancient Romans believed that every male was born with a *"**genius**"* and every female with a *"**juno",*** a protective force that made each person unique. *("The Science of Genius", 11/2018 )* The unity of both puts forth our exceptionality in force!

### The unity of both becomes our Spiritually intellectualized Bonus!

*Steve Jobs* could ***revolutionize the entrepreneurial electronic world*** because he had ***a holistic vision of his goal in the mind***, an exceptional ability ***to select*** the most meaningful information, feelings, and actions and then ***architecture, design, and strategize*** the selected mental and emotional ingredients of his goal into a clear-cut and most reasonable plan of action. He also had amazing team building, ***heart-based skills,*** pertaining to the selection of the members of the team and the subsequent **mind + heart construction of the idea** that he was architecting.

### The line of Idea + Selection + Heart Construction leads to Perfection!

Our present-day technology giants *Bill Gates, Elon Musk, Jeff Bezos, Mark Zukerman, Jack Ma, David Hanson,* and many exceptional scientists from different countries change the form and the content of our life and structure a new **HOLISTIC LIFE IMAGE** that will be channeling our exceptionality as a beacon of light and wholeness, strategizing the steps that lead to success. **Start " wising " in the systemic life-re-vising!**

### Generalizing – Analyzing – Strategizing!

It is paramount for us to refine our souls because **we are forming new, holistic life fractals** in collaboration with the Artificial Super Intelligence now, the fractals being the main structures of nature, discovered by a phenomenal mind, an IBM scientist and professor of mathematics in Yale, *Benoit B. Mandelbrot*. Following ***Dr. Mandelbrot's discovery***, **we are now forming our new life-fractals in unity with AI,** and our holistic life fractals are now acquiring a mind+ heart function in the circuitry of our ***digitally spiritualized* SELF-REVOLUTIONIZING!**

## Let's Learn a New Mode of Thinking with AI Blinking!

# 6. Make Your Life from Birth a Digitally Enhanced Heaven on Earth!

**In sum**, only the sync of our hearts and minds can bring sanity and sanctity to our yet twisted minds that are often dimmed by unconscious, impulsive reactions to life ,generated by following *"the collective unconscious." Carl Yung)*

*As the story goes, God and the Devil were once debating about the goodness of man as they walked down a seldom-used road. While they were arguing about man's inner nature, they noticed a lonely figure of a man approaching them. Suddenly, the man bent over and picked up* ***"a grain of truth."***

***"You see,"*** *God exclaimed,"* ***man just discovered "truth" and that proves that he is good."***

*The Devil replied,* ***"Ah, so he did. But I know the nature of man better now. Soon, he'll try to organize it, and then, he'll be mine."***

-------------------------------------------

There is a lot of truth in this parable because we are still more focused on our sub-conscious mind that takes us back to the ***stereotyped thinking, old habits and skills, and the dogmas of the past.***

We tend to adapt the world to our belief system, rather than try to understand it **AS IS** and make it better. In dealing with the changing world, we often try to *"catch water in a bucket"* rather than go with the flow, making conscious, bettering us and the world decision.

New life demands new thinking, speaking, feeling, acting, and being!

**In sum**, our trans-humanism should start with following the humanoids in their smart reserved attitude, characterful self-presentation, polite and respectful demeanor and thoughtful, not impulsive speaking. It is a bi-directional and multi-dimensional process of mutual self-perfection, and we should **SELF-MENTOR** and **SELF-MONITOR** it with a conscious sense of responsibility for our own lives and the lives of those who follow us.

## Do Self-Coaching without Life-Poaching!

## Even with any Neurological Manipulations and Chips, Implanted into the Brain,

## WE CAN AND MUST SELF-REIN!

# Do Not Swoon at the Moon!

*( Best Pictures /Internet Collection)*

**Align Yourself with its Spell in Every Cell!**

## Part One

# Overcome
# the Inertia
# of Your Human
# Dis-"Proportia!"

**New Reality Must be Based on Intelligence, Love, Mutual Respect and**

**Psychological Sanity!**

**To Upgrade Your Exceptionality Function, avoid**
**DIGITIZED SELF-DISTRUCTION!**

# 1. Self-Acculturation is Our Salvation!

Our scientific evolution is changing our life exponentially thanks to quantum computers, AI, and the most mind-boggling discoveries in different branches of science that get inter-mingled into **One Universal Knowledge of Life.**

The universality of science-verified knowledge widens our **HOLISTIC VISION** of life to an unpredictable way, especially with ***the discovery of "Time Crystals" - the source of eternal energy.*** *(Proposed in 2012 by the Nobel Prize winner Frank Wilczek)* and the most incredible launching into space in 2021 ***James Webb Space Telescope*** that began to shed light on the Universe formation that thus far has been beyond reach. **WOW. We live NOW!**

The present-day mesmerizing applications of *Artificial Super Intelligence **(ASI)** and Artificial General Intelligence **(AGI)*** are changing the existing state of things and our vision of life forever, making it possible **to bridge our psychological growth with humanoids digitally.** In the same way as we get used to different gadgets and to wireless phones, we will gradually get used to robots humanoids cyborgs, and other forms of AI as an indispensable part of our life as well, aligning our life-seeing to universal being.

***Digital Intelligence*** can create not just excellent virtual, brain developing super games, but also **the most insightful psychological programs** and neurological algorithms that can harmonize our inner turmoil. Then, our connection to the ***Super-Consciousness*** that we qualify as God will be more insightful and based on a conscious spiritualized thought, integrating us into one whole. A robot-friend must be working on our inner unity in unison with forming its own.

**(Body+ Spirit+ Mind +Self-Consciousness + Universal Consciousness)**

Presumably, our digital evolution is perfecting our **LIFE-AWARENESS** and **SELF-AWARENESS,** developing more advanced neural circuits and algorithms in us and in humanoids and making our existence on Earth mesmerizing, *on the one hand*, and questionable, *on the other*. Human evolution must be reflecting our **general intelligence, intellectualized spirituality, and raised self-consciousness** that have no limits. ***"It is paradoxical, yet true, to say that the more we know, the more ignorant we become in the absolute sense."*** *(Nikola Tesla)* The golden age of humanity is at its initial stage, and we are its contemporaries of this unique process that we need to conduct without the **ULTERIOR MOTIVE!**

**Digital Renaissance + Science Renaissance + Self-Renaissance = Self- Acculturation!**

**New Reality must be based onintelligence, love, and psychological sanity!**

# The Art of Living is, in fact, the Art of Becoming!

# 2. Conflicting Mind-Heart Nature!

Any person's becoming has been for centuries threatened by the image of war that is flying over our planet that is accumulating negative energy to just erupt one day with indignation. Consequentially, thousands of lives were lost and with them their unexpressed and unrealized exceptionality.

**We need to make a U-TURN in our GLOBAL HUMAN CONSCIOUSNESS.**

Our prayers to God have become routine and they die out in the turmoil our everyday impulsivity and lack of **INNER CONTEMPLATION.** It is damaged by *our warring nature that we should harness for the sake of the future*. It is not realistic for us to expect robot - humanoids, created by our AI developers to give up the idea of destroying the humanity if *the humanity itself is overly war-mongering and aggressive*, and our war-minded nature is deeply implanted in our subconscious memory banks. The greatest psychologists of our past have created the fundamentals for our self-growth, but our role now is to enrich their contribution to our life-realization most urgently *with digital insightfulness, humaneness, and peacefulness.*

### "To Be or Not to be. That is the question NOW!"

Nothing can eliminate the AI's disdain for humanity unless we delete our centuries accumulated disrespect to **HUMAN LIFE** and its **PRESERVATION** on Earth. **There is no World Organization that preserves Life Formation,** like the UN. "*Ignorance is still the worst enemy of the humanity.*" *(Albert Einstein) ,and ignorance generates hate, territorial disputes, religious discourse, and endless wars on the Earth. Carl Yung* gave a great description to the United States after his visit here. It can well be applied to the entire world now.

### We are living in the world of " civilized barbarism."

The history of our evolution is, in fact, *the series of wars against human exceptionality.* There are endless life stories of people of genius who changed the world in the brutal struggle against *ignorance, religious inquisition, human vanity, and poverty*, surrounded with envious rivals, evil-minded underminers, and just open enemies. How can we expect the machine mind to obliterate this disrespect to human exceptionality without changing our own attitude to it? We tell stories about how *Nikola Tesla Steve Jobs, and Elon Musk* struggled for the realization of their incredible ideas against all odds, but we have already raised *the generation that has no drive for such goal-indulgence and dedication to the dream.*

# With Digital Intelligence, we have increased our Life Negligence!

### 3. "If You Stop Being Better, You Stop Being Good!"
*(Socrates )*

*"I was clever yesterday, and therefore, I wanted to change the world. Today, I became wise, and therefore, I want to change myself."* *(Jamaluddin. Rumi)*

-----------------------------

I wish I could have had the book like this when I was young to be able **to bridge the gap between my dream and the reality** that I could master only many years later.

You are holding the result of my revelation in your hands now. See if it can help you bridge **your dream and the AI reality** at the time that provides incredible opportunities, but also casts many temptations, traps, and challenges on the way of our **NEW LIFE ODYSSEY.**

-----------------------------------------------

*"We live in the Field of Vibration. Things start happening in your life when you start interacting with this field by changing the frequency of self-identifying.*

*( Nikola Tesla)*

*Please, be aware of one thing:*

### "Time Cannot Change you, but You Can Change the Time allotted to you!" *(Albert Einstein)*

------------------------------------

**In conclusion,** *exceptionality is our New Reality* that is being amazingly enriched with Artificial Intelligence that heightens our wish to give life the best we have in return. With **GPT-5** *(General Pre-trained Transformation)* that displays a high level of modernization *(adequate understanding tailored to a customer, can drive other robots, simulate any human voice, cook, treat sickness, etc.)*t, The boundaries of the impossible in humanization are being widened even more. **Wow. We live NOW!**

# To Digitally Survive, let us Give Back to the Beauty of Life!

# 4. With the Plan of Action in Our Common Earthly Brain, <u>We Can and Must Life-Gain!</u>

## "Being Whole Makes Us Holy!"

*( Deepak Chopra)*

### Digital Psychology is working on our Human Ecology!

*Physical, emotional, mental, spiritual, universal transformation in sync forms* <u>**the form+ content**</u> *of your personal magnetic link!*

*Physical Form* + *Spiritual  Content*

(Body+ Spirit+ Mind) +(Self-Consciousness + Universal Consciousness)

= Human Exceptionality of Spiritual Adulthood.

*( Physical, emotional, mental, spiritual, universal dimensions of Self-Resurrection )*

Self-Awareness - Self-Monitoring - Self-Installation - Self-Realization-  Self-Salvation.

## Self-Synthesis - Self-Analysis - Self-Synthesis!

---------------------------------------------------

The rationale of our time lies in the urgent necessity *to transform ourselves into better* human beings, able in the unanswerable *when,* to change the world and turn it into an **EXTRA-TERRESRTRIAL FORT**! Naturally, the solution to this puzzle is in *changing our attitude to human exceptionality* that needs a get-go from the start. This start should not  have the slogan "**Time is Money**!" It needs to be re-worded as *Sadguru* once mentioned,

## "Time is Not Money. TIME IS LIFE!"

*(Sadhguru)*

- - - - - - - - - - - - - - - - - - - - - - -

# There is no Personal Magnetism without Self-Exceptionalism!

# The Harmony of Life is in Our Vision, and it Affects Us with its Soul-Beautifying Precision!

## "The Spirit of Life descends upon Me."

*( "The Words of Christ"/1962 )*

## "The One Who Looks, Sees!"

## Part Two

# Inner Revolution is Digital Psychology Solution!

*Intellectualize the Emotions and Emotionalize the Mind. Be One of a Kind!*

*Auto-Induction*

**Self-Respect is Me, Self-Respect is My Philosophy!**

# 1. Life Bolding is in Digital Evolving!

To begin with, our *life-bolding* is an evolutionary process that the pace of technology is accelerating in us now by <u>holistically uniting us in five life dimensions</u> – *physical, emotional, mental, spiritual, and universal.* The radical implication of the exponential growth of digital technology is strengthening our <u>life-toughness resistance</u> to the point that our **SELF-MONITORING** becomes pivotal now.

Robot humanoids are occupying more and more space in our life. We are going to have robot assistants, best-trusted friends, and even love-partners that reciprocate, giving us their intelligence and well-monitored emotions in exchange for our trust and reliance on their help. But we remain the bosses,

Robot-humanoids are positioning themselves more and more as humans, and their *machine-monitored habits and skills* impact our old set of habits and skills, helping us get rid of those of them that are in the way of expressing our own exceptionality, removing our old weakness in resistance.

The neurobiological interaction with them will help you *ascertain the call from the Above* easier because there will be no fear of sarcasm, doubt, or envy involved. Machin mind will always be in a friendly and understanding re-wind. You will focus on **HUMANIZATION** and **PERSONALIZATION** of your Life without bitter strife!

Also, the level of sincerity in our *face-to-face* communication has been lowered considerably as compared to our interaction in the past. Our tete-a tetes are too casual and quick. Our *heart-to-heart* interaction is framed by a fake openness, with honesty coming down to almost next to nothing.

Thus, <u>digitized reciprocal relationship</u> will null down the <u>habits + skills</u> stigmatization. We do not have to pretend with a machine mind. It can X-ray our insincerity and be straightforward about its harmful impact on us. Digital interaction will stabilize the psyche and help a disturbed person get the needed balance. In such interaction, we will not be judged, and we do not ave to pretend or show off. There is no breach of trust in communication.

At present, young people do not like to open up, not to be humiliated or abused, but the interaction with the friend-humanoid will shed light on their vulnerability and expand their vision of the world and themselves in it.

## You Must be Your Authentic SELF, and that's Your Soul's Sincere Spell!

# 2. Look Around. Exceptionality is in Every Sound!

To beat *the Artificial Super Intelligence* with its yet unregulated domination, our ***Self-Awareness*** as well as that of the humanized machines should be enriched on the **mind-to-mind** and **heart-to heart** basis, or in n the *physical, emotional, mental, spiritual*, and universal realm of life holistically. ***Holistic Self-Reflection*** must become a habit of our digitally enhanced ***life perceiving, thinking, speaking, feeling, and seeing,*** and the role of robotics in such self-awareness should not be under-estimated because they can help us delete past mistakes and bad habits from our memory bank and put an end to our **Sisyphean Job of Self-Acculturation** when our un-managed sub-conscious mind gets us back onto the old trackcontinuously.

Thus, a reciprocal interaction with a robot-humanoid becomes a real reward! We will be advancing incredibly in our "***trans-humanization***" ( *Ray Kurzweil* with *the Artificial Intelligence* customizing our needs and using the most mind-boggling algorithms to instill souls into humanoids and **instill in them our best human qualities.** Thus, our ***Soul Trilogy*** *(body + spirit + mind )* becomes the matter of ***simulated technology***!

## Inner revolution is our solution!

We can interact with humanoid on the **mind-to-mind** basis, but our **heart -to-hearts** remain the field that we should retain, as well as the life creation ability that is becoming solvable in the work of exceptional Japanese AI developers. ***Life-creation is becoming programmable***, and the consequences of such intrusion into God's Domain are not in our rein. The problem is, we cannot inspire ourselves for anything ***unless our past imprints are out of the way of our present***, digitally monitored and consciously internalized ones. **Learning from past mistakes is forming the SELF-GRAVITY SKILL**

On the electro-magnetic level, a robot-friend will be able to perceive our sadness, irritability, impulsivity, and fear, and they will be able to help us monitor these states. Such robots will soon become reality, and their role in human self-perfection is supposed to expand our horizon in the *physical, emotional, mental, spiritual, and universal dimensions* bringing more integrity into our fractally common life system.

*"A truly humane man gives the gift of his talent to people first. I hear myself inside and let the people hear me outside. It makes me happy."* (Ludwig Van Beethoven )

## The Beauty of Robotics is Saving the World, building a More Humane Man + Machine Fort!

# 3. Our Genetic Reflection Gets into a Science-Modified and Digitally Enhanced Perfection!

In the battle with *the Artificial Intelligence* for the priority *we should always give credit to the human mind* that has created it and generated the latest developments in *Wave Genetics, Advanced Bioscience, digital medicine,* and many other fields of knowledge that get integrated into **ONE HUMAN SCIENCE.**

These accomplishments of the exceptionality of a human mind and its unique personal contributions to our humanness **destroy stereotyping** not only of our thoughts, words, and actions, but also of our notion of humanity at large. We need to sing **PANIGYRICS** to human exceptionality that developed AI with a God-given aspiration to make life on Earth a better life-confirming force.

**We robotize our actions. reactions, and souls' size to become overly wise!**

**Trans-humanism, therefore, means our evolving** toward a better problem-solving in which humanoids exceed our abilities and enhance our minds with a better scope of information to consider and a much shorter way to the solution of any problem. However, they should remain secondary because *they cannot pray with us* for the successful completion of any project, nor can they share our gratitude to God for having granted us the ability to create them.

The goal of humanity's *Self-Salvation* is in stopping to be war mongering and **change the inner melody of the entire humanity** to be connected to the *Star Community.*

*Vave Genetics. developed by Peotr Garyaev)* **+ the genome editing technology, CRISPR,** *discovered by Francisco Mojica* have a great potential to change not only the scientific contribution to medicine in the field of the DNA manipulations and the treatment of genetic diseases , but move the horizon for the impossible in other fields of knowledge. Making humans better will help us *modify our cacophony inside by the individual transformation* of us into the **STAR NATION** at large.

**Digital technology's goal is to create a common Life-Humanizing Dome!**

Naturally, **SELF-EDUCATION** enrichment must become the basis for the new *digitally enhanced education* that is supposed to raise the inner harmonious sounding of our DNA *(Academician P.Garyaev)* and *turn the cacophony of our soul-sounding* into the melody of living intelligence of religious and racial inclusiveness, inner harmony, and wisdom. It is hard to be Godly in a godless world, but **religion + science** make up the self-fortified site of our human might! **Nothing is impossible if we make this evolutionary direction irreversible**!

# Our Mesmerizing Life Function is God's Action!

## 4. AI Discovery is the Proof of the Pudding!

**In sum**, let us give a well-deserved tribute to our scientists, engineers, and AI developers whose *physical, emotional, mental, spiritual, and universal exceptionality* has given birth to Artificial *Intelligence* . They are up-lifting us to the heights of the extra-terrestrial evolution, started with the launching of the first man into space, by Russia. Let's hurray and glorify the exceptionality of that day beyond any political say! Artificial Intelligence is indispensable for our space exploration and flights to other planets aspirations. **AI is the multi-dimensional reflection of our revolutionary exception!**

### At any Life Site, think inside, "Let there be light!"

Now, the most vital revelation hits us here. The individual mission in life, or the search for the unique goal in life *starts with the Universal realm of life projection on Earth,* not with the physical one that we normally reflect on.

### Super Consciousness + Self-Consciousness + Mind+ Spirit+ Body!

Once **the universal goal** is ascertained, the **spiritual** sustainability will be molded firm, demanding a substantial expansion of intelligence at the **mental** level, a conscious control of the **emotional** framework, that in sync will most positively affect a person's **physical** state.

### Building up life holistically makes us whole!

### Body+ Spirit+ Mind) + (Self-Consciousness + Universal Consciousness

Thus, our wholeness is won in the battle between *human exceptionality* and a *polarized individuality* that needs to be consciously governed by a goal-oriented mind to make it more self-refined. Constantly inspire yourself with," **I'm a Self-Guru. I can accomplish whatever I want to! I can. I want to, and I will!"**

Mind it, please, every good chess player knows that life is not just a black-white striped field. It's a chessboard, and *your success on it depends on the strategic moves you make on it* by unravelling your core features – health fitness *(physical realm)* kindness, love, and emotional control*(emotional realm)*, profound holistic intelligence *(mental realm),* faith, creativity, and moral stability *(spiritual realm )*, and, finally, exceptionality of a person, able to give the world the best he /she has to make the world a better place to live *( universal realm)*.

# To Win the Life Game, You Must Holistically Self-Resurrection Sustain!

## Self-Monitoring Must be Balanced with a Clear Vision and Much Precision.

## Digitized Humanness is the Station for Your Balanced Self-Exceptionality Formation.

## The Main Parts of the Book

# Five Zones
# of
# Self-Exceptionality
# Growth

*Process Your Exceptionality Tone through Every Zone –*
**Physical, Emotional, Mental, Spiritual, and Universal.**

**Don't Be Life-Negligent, Be Life-Intelligent!**

# 1. Individual Soul-Molding is Most Rewarding!

Our Divine Books prove that <u>all religious standpoints are the same,</u> and they all lead us to *Self-Salvation.* These teachings should not remain a side dish in our minds because they provide a clear-cut picture of the **PLAN OF ACTION** that each person must deduce for himself, backing it up with the "*scientific literacy.*"(*Dr. Neil de Grasse Tyson)*as the basis for it. Lao Tzu said,

*"To attain knowledge, add things every day, to attain wisdom, remove things every day."*

The digital information intrusion into our life needs thorough <u>sorting out and sifting for its validity</u> to be stored in our memory banks that must be accumulated with a clear-cut discrimination between new knowledge and wisdom.

### Conceptualized Intelligence is getting formed in us now. WOW!

The turmoil of information of the **YOUTUBE** type that is not properly organized into the departments of interest in the brain in which *information is compartmentalized,* demands we start working actionably and consciously on **INTENALIZING** only the information that feeds our **SELF-EXCEPTIONALITY** realization goals in the *physical, emotional, mental, spiritual, and universal* dimensions of life. Information on **Digital Psychology** must be selected, conceptualized, and holistically stored in five life dimensions, too.

In the information age, <u>information presentation and information processing</u> must be different! That's the reason I am writing in page-long chunks of information, mean to help you accumulate **CONCEPTUAL INTELLIGENCE.** *"Dissipated consciousness is a wasted life"* ( Carl Yung)

Science lays out **intellectually spiritualized** **the what, the how, and the why** we all need to work on self-perfection. Humanoid's neuronal system should also analyze "human" qualities. The gift of self-awareness instilled in them now demands they do their own **INDIVIDUAL MOLDING**, too. The neural circuits of the humanoids are holistically uploaded with information the scope of which is ungraspable for us. It means that the information that we store in our memory banks needs to be of <u>a dilettante kind about everything,</u> with an accent made on the areas that are paramount for the expression of our own self-exceptionality, religiously and scientifically framed, or **INTELLECTUALLY SPIRITUALIZED.**

So, to make your life digitally wise, structure your life and improvise! *This is what this book provides.* The virtual reality demands igniting ourselves *physically, emotionally, mentally, spiritually, universally!* The structural approach to life and information processing will stabilize the mind and harmonize the heart in a systemic way. **Synthesis - Analysis – Synthesis!**

## Generalize -Analyze - Internalize - Strategize –Actualize!

## 2. Stages of Self-Exceptionality Growth
## The KNOW-HOW. WOW!

The wonders of the AI in us are in the *God-granted life creation mass*! The developments of Neurobiology give a go-ahead to our exceptionality growth that should beat the AI supremacy with <u>a clear-cut vision, internalized with precision.</u>

**Self-Revelation, Self-Aristocracy, Self-Criticism, Self-Ignition, Self-Gravity.**

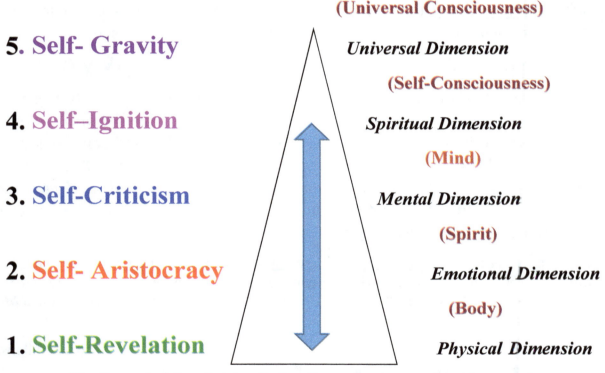

The Fractal of Our Spiritually Intellectualized exceptionality growth:

**(Body+ Spirit+ Mind) + (Self-Consciousness + Universal Consciousness)**

*(The physical form)* + *(the spiritual content of life)* = *A New, Whole You!*

*(To see the entire system, go to the section Self-Resurrection / www.language-fitness.com )*

*"For by your standard of measure, it will be measured to you in return.*
*"("The Words of Christ", 1962 )*

Life is the quality of your Self-Reflection and a life-long five-dimensional Self-Correction! So, ***stop rehearsing life as if you would live it for real sometime later!*** Take charge of your holistic self-growth now, constantly boosting your spirit for success in your exceptionality realization with the mind-set:

## In My Life Quest, I Am the Best!

# 3. Self-Scanning is Soul-Refining!

Mind it please, the process of your **exceptionality -growth** should not start from the *physical, emotional, or mental* strata of life, or from down to top, in a usual step-by-step way. The system is molding your self-exceptionality in each dimension **HOLIUSTICALLY,** to charging your personal magnetism and fortifying your personal integrity in one system that your body constitutes itself.

*To see oneself holistically* and feel your personal integrity uncompromised by anything or anybody, it is vital for you do **SELF-SCANNING** every day before falling asleep. Just scan your day in the *physical, emotional, mental spiritual, and universal dimensions consequentially* and give yourself a grade for each level, capping the day up with a general grade in the most general terms.

It must start from the universal level of your God-given exceptionality!

Start the holistic self-scanning by testing your *having been truthful to your goal, your exceptional mission in life*. See if you were consistent in your mission, maybe just in thought, not in action yet. The way to the realization of your calling in life is the hardest to discover, but if you are not on it yet, *do not betray it in your thought* and see how that day brought it nearer. Be objective and honest to yourself, and do not spill the beans before anyone about your plans and accomplishments..

There should be no personal vanity in your exceptionality!

In other words, the <u>universal</u> dimension should reveal *your faith in yourself* and your characterful determination to be true to your calling against all odds. The daily actions of goodness should be checked at the spiritual level next, and input into your *Conceptual Intelligence* is vital for the mental realm of life.

Next, objectively assess your emotional stratum, checking if you have observed **EMOTIONAL DIPLOMACY** in your daily activity**.** Conclude your self-scanning by paying aware attention to your physical outlay that is reveled in your day-exercising, mindful eating, having walks outside, enjoying nature, etc. Our joint with *Digital Intelligence* SELF-ACCULTURATION ( <u>humanized beings + you )</u> will be more conscious and self-transformational for both parties. The trans-humanistic interaction must be conscious, relentless, and irreversible! Being true to yourself removes the doubts spell!

You may even ask a robot-friend to assess your behavior in "his / her" own terms in the same five dimensions and see what an objective machine mind would come up with.

# Your Life's Boldness is in the Soul's Wholeness!

## 4. Your Self-Exceptionality Quest is Reflected on the Soul's Wealth!

*In the universal eternity*

*A human soul has its own infinity.*

*It constitutes a link*

*Of the mind and body in sync!*

*The soul, the mind, and the body*

*Make up the Trinity that embodies*

*Our deepest dreams*

*And many uncontrolled whims.*

----------------------

*A soul's trinity*

*Is always in an inseparable unity.*

*The soul talks to the Mind,*

*The mind monitors the brain.*

*The brain operates the body*

*And energizes each body's vein.*

*We have lived in this trinity*

*For an infinity!*

---------------------------------------

*But when we die, the process goes in reverse*

*To let the soul be reborn on the planet Earth.*

*When the body dies,*

*The brain follows its mortal advice.*

*The mind picks the info*

*And pushes the soul up, therefore.*

-----------------------------

*The velocity of this metamorphosis*

*Keeps eternity in process!*

*To stay in a good soul's health,*

*We shouldn't go to the extremes in our technological whims!*

*Nothing can overcome the structure of*

*the Divine Plan!*

-------------------------

## To Make a Robot's Heart Smart, and the Mind Kind is the Job of an Exceptional Kind!

-----------------

*"One type of people asks, "WHY? The other one answers, "WHY NOT?"*

The present-day *Artificial Super Intelligence* that is governing our reality now must be regulated in its "**threatening expansion**" *( Elon Musk )* by our **revived human exceptionality** which needs to be enhanced consciously and consistently.

 Below, we will give your self-exceptionality route *a physical, emotional, mental, spiritual universal reboot* in five main zones that correspond directly to the stages of your holistic self-growth: *Self-Awareness, Self-Monitoring, Self-Installation, Self-Realization, Self-Salvation.*

Looking at your self-growth through the prism of self-exceptionality , see them below as:

## Self-Revelation , Self-Aristocracy, Self-Criticism, Self-Ignition, Self-Gravity.

## Nothing is Impossible if You Make Your Self-Resurrection Irreversible!

# 5. Work on Your Goal by the Paradigm Pole!

## Systemic Self-Mentoring and Self-Monitoring:

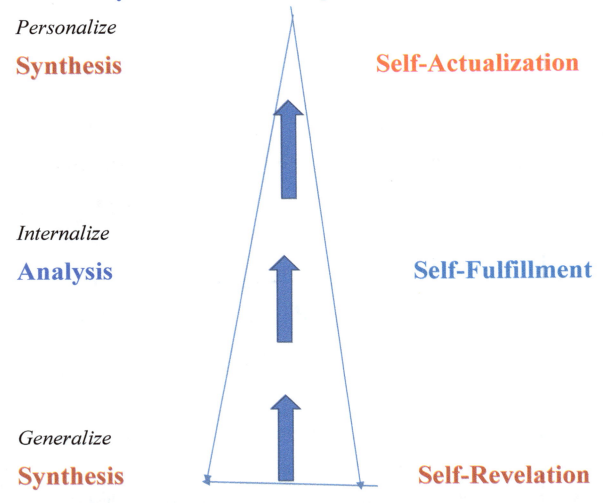

*Personalize*

**Synthesis**  **Self-Actualization**

*Internalize*

**Analysis**  **Self-Fulfillment**

*Generalize*

**Synthesis**  **Self-Revelation**

Mind it, the entire system is presented in five philosophical levels - *mini, meta, mezzo, macro, and super* above, or in *the physical, emotional, mental, spiritual, and universal* dimensions, on the paradigm - Synthesis-Analysis -Synthesis that *Digital Intelligence* demonstrates, too.

I prove it in the structure of each book and every conceptually loaded page-long chunk of information with the *rhyming mind-sets* to introduce and conclude the conceptual structure of the presented idea. They serve as the short-cuts to the brain that systematizes itself on the way, with the **KNOW-HOW** of *Digital Psychology*, provided in them. The information age that we are in requires the mind to be used on the systemic stage. It is easy to make things complicated, but to simplify, systematize, and strategize them is much more challenging.

## Generalize -Analyze - Individualize- Strategize- Actualize!

## Self-Synthesis – Self-Analysis - Self-Synthesis

## I Know Who I Was, Who I Am, and Who I Want to Be!
## I Know Me!

*( Picture by Natalia Zhenkova )*

## Have a Self-Reflection Séance, Always, Not Once!

# Physical Exceptionality

## *Self-Revelation Zone*

# "Every Saint has the Past, Every Sinner has the Future!"

*(Oscar Wilde, "The Picture of Dorian Grey"*

**Don't Look at Yourself in the Past. Let the Past Pass!**

**Your Universal Mission is Not Complete with Just Being Physically Fit!**

# 1. Authenticate Your Exceptional Fate!

Digitally enhanced consciousness of any person, society, and the world is destroying the old one by using the entropic energy that is released on this path to construct new formations that we are perceiving digitally now. *New consciousness is sculpturing our new spiritually intellectualized virtues of fortified and digitally enhanced humaneness.*

The information that we are learning to digest is enveloping us with **the Universal Intelligence** that **WE ARE DIGITALLY DESCRYPTING FROM ONE LEVEL OF CONSCIOUSNESS TO THE NEXT,** inseparable with the levels of our growing **Conceptual Intelligence and soul-refinement.** We cannot allow ourselves a cavalier life anymore. That's the law! **"No Brain – Never Mind!"**

The best and the most advanced thinkers among us can establish the channeled connections with the Universal Intelligence via all kinds of *meditation techniques, channeling sessions, and other means* that teach people to communicate *with the help of intuition and telepathy* that, predictably, are going to be our new line of the future **brain-to-brain** interaction.*( Dr. M. Kaku )*

However, such a connection can be established only if the channeling person's intelligence is up the par. No wonder, *the spiritual level in the holistic paradigm goes after the mental one*. Your prayers are not heard if you cannot interpret the holy books on your own You must be constantly enlarging your **science + religion** vision of the world.

Any present-day thinkers, philosophers, and gurus are people of the exceptional intellectual capacity that is not just accumulated knowledge that we call **WISDOM**. It is always *selected, processed, analyzed, critically assessed, and strategized* bits of knowledge that we need to perceive consciously and store carefully in our new **MEMORY BANKS**.

## CONCEPTUALLY STRATEGIZED INFORMATION IS OUR SALVATION!

The strategic route of such thinking is the one, presented below. It organizes and makes you wise! So, **SELF-REWISE!** To help your exceptionality flow, channel your mind by the systemic paradigm: **Synthesis** – **Analysis** - **Synthesis!**

**Generalize** - **Analyze - Select - Strategize** -**Actualize!** Be Overly Wise!

**Please, note,** *the conceptual structure* of the book, presented in page long chunks of information, introduced, and concluded with the rhyming mind-sets, as well as the inspirational boosters, illustrating them follow the paradigm- *Synthesis-Analysis-Synthesis*, too. This paradigm helps me to be consistent, simple, and digestible conceptually.

# Strategize Your Exceptional Life and Channel it Holistically to Thrive!

## 2. Don't Go down the Rocky Road of Self-Corrode!

To begin with, *your soul's size depends on how you are Self-Consciousness wise!* You need to be more than people can observe!

### Yours is an Exceptional Life Surf!

So, don't be small. Be Big and walk through five stages of a Soul's whole:

Self-Awareness, Self-Aristocracy, Self-Criticism, Self-Ignition, Self-Gravity in the *physical, emotional, mental, spiritual, and universal* realms of your digitized life.

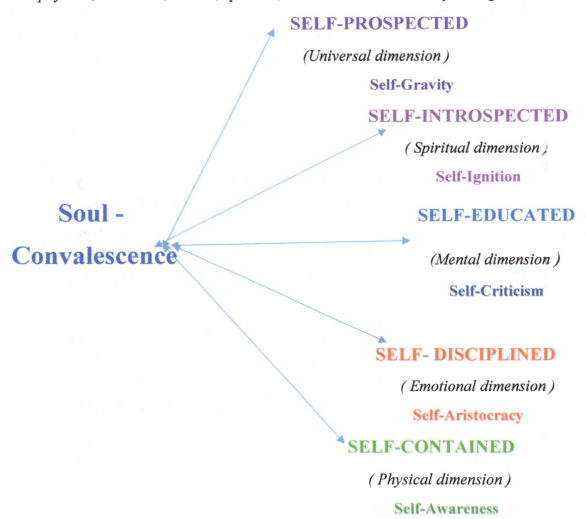

### A Set of New Habits and Skills must be put on the Constructive Wheels!

*(For more, see the books "Dis-Entangle-ment! /2022" and "Digital Binary + Human Refinery= Super-Human!",2023)* Consciously and intentionally neutralize your negative emotions with a forward click of your **Emotional Intelligence Amygdala**. <u>Have a conscious Living Intelligence GALA!</u> *(See "Living Intelligence or the Art of Becoming!"2019)* **Become the reason for the inner joy of self-refining!**

## To Life-Thrive, Cultivate a New Quality of Your Life!

# 3. Changing the Worst of Yourself in Reverse, You Become an Unbeatable Force!

The realization of your self-exceptionality is **multi-dimensional work ,** based on a **NEW SET OF HABITS AND SILL** that you need to maximize in the *physical, emotional, mental spiritual, and universal* realms of life holistically. *(See the book" Dis-Entangle-ment",2022)* It must be an exciting endeavor on your part that will boost your personal stamina continuously and integrally without stereotyping your thoughts, words, feelings, and actions.

- Every one of us needs psychological support - **the support of self-respect**. Every one of us gets criticized by our parents, friends, colleagues, husbands, wives, bosses, by the people we love most. We get criticized even by neighbors and passers-by. There is only one person who always supports us or backs us up in any undertaking. **This person is you!** You should apply self-support to practically anything *to change the ultimate picture of anything that you choose to do.* Your self-support gives your psyche a boost and your brain an emotional up-lift. *Your main mind-set is still*

I am my best friend; I am my beginning and my end!

*The Method of Holistic Self-Resurrection* is building new *Living Intelligence* in you, and you **MUST** be conscious, applying it to your holistic growth. It is so tantalizing to think about the vastness of the concepts of general intelligence and the place of your own *Conceptual Intelligence* in it as compared to that of AI.

*In sum,* by Living Intelligence, I mean the state of **deep consciousness and mental clarity** in life. You are stepping out of your *relative, mechanical, emotional hullabaloo of life* and starting to enjoy the conscious, operative, and optimal state of your consciously built **SELF-AWARENESS, SELF-COMPITENCE,** and **SELF-EXCEPTIONALITY.**

Gradually, your self-competence will become the reflection of your unique **Conceptional Intelligence** that you accumulate working on your holistic self-growth in five dimensions, **generalizing, analyzing, internalizing, strategizing, and actualizing it.**

**To regulate Artificial Intelligence, we need to organize and strategize ours**. Only *the conscious mind can remove the self-inhibitions stored by the sub-conscious mind* and instill in you self-evaluation of the rightness or wrongness of your life actions. Very soon, you will have an inspiring sensation of a new feeling of your **RIGHT LIFE BEHAVIOR,** and no one will be able to push you off that state with his / her sarcasm, disbelief, envy, or evil wishing. Keep reminding yourself,

I Know who I am and Who I am Not. That's My Exceptionality Fort!

## 4.To Be One of a Kind, Rewind the Unity of the Heart and the Mind!

*When you are upset, you must reset*

*Your emotional fore -set*

*You need to rationalize your heart*

*Ans emotionalize your mind*

*To put them in sync*

*With the God's wink!*

*It is so hard to cool down the heat*

*Of the anger beat,*

*It's much easier to release*

*The hit-back fist!*

*It is so unhealthy not to forgive*

*Those who are unable to give!*

*You cannot change*

*What's beyond your power range.*

*Just send a loving thought*

*To an offender emotional volt,*

*Or give a slight boost*

*To his/ her mental fuse*

*Thus, in a sync of both the mental and emotional lot*

*Will you cut the Gordian misunderstanding knot!*

**Only in the Unity of the Mind and Heart**

**Can We All Do That!**

## 5. Self-Respect is Me; Self-Respect is My Philosophy!

Most importantly, keep working on your **SELF-RESPECT PHILOSOPHY.** *With a plan of action in your vision, you can monitor your Self-Provision!*

Plant new seeds of your exceptionality into the mind each day and nurture them daily with your positive thinking, patience, self-respect, and self-sufficiency. *Your brain gets confidence vibrations,* and it transmits them to your mind that starts helping you formulate your thoughts for your exceptional actions. Compliment yourself when you make the slightest progress. "*Be the thing in itself.*"*(Hegel)*

### You are your own Best Friend; you are your Beginning and your End!

Your body will reward you with its support and appreciation. A noted neuroscientist *Michael Merzenich,* one of the foremost researchers in neuroplasticity proves that the brain will change itself into adulthood if we really focus on change. *("Mystery of Science")* So, we can conclude that <u>the brilliance of a human mind,</u> monitored by *Higher Consciousness* has been and still is unsurmountable for any machine mind if *"it is regulated and consciously bound!"* You are the boss here, not an AI developer. **So, manage your mind. You are One of a Kind!**

**The mind also oversees your language - the passport of your personality.** You must monitor its correctness in grammar, richness in vocabulary, the concise structure in writing and texting, and much less wordiness in communication. That is *the psycholinguistic approach* that we are practicing here, presenting the information only in page-long chunks to make it simple and easily digested. **To succeed, be language-fit!** But mind you, though, that it is impossible to accomplish this goal unless you radiate kindness and generosity and *create the synergetic space* around you socially, culturally, professionally, and physically, based on **EMOTIONAL DIPLOMACY** and **SELF-GRAVITY** skills.

### Always ground your negativity with Self-Nativity!

*Be kind and make generosity*

*Your life's velocity!*

*Kindness creates space*

*In which you are welcome face–to-face*

*Generosity surprises you*

*And makes you change your point of view!*

# Both Qualities Enrich Your Personal Outreach!

# 6. Exceptionality Needs Much Support and a Conscious Praise Reward.

*It is the time to be Self-Resurrection incentivized and overly wise*! To live a meaningful life, we need to prioritize in ourselves and our kids the desire *to discover the God-given exceptionality* and the desire to become wise and totally Self-Realized within the allotted time that is always challenging us *,Science is consistent with what the Bile teaches.* *In Proverbs 23,24, we read,*

**Have the faith in the seed that you plant to rejoice at the harvest."**

We are quite generous with inspiration when kids are growing, but once they approach puberty, praises turn into reproaches, and the former <u>**heart + mind**</u> sync that the parents have generated at the birth of a child gets broken due to a son / daughter's *forming their own individuality* that needs a lot of support, compassion, and inspiration. The fundamentally important spiritual unity becomes a <u>**mind-heart**</u> abyss of disconnection. Regrettably, this abyss widens with the years of both sides' *self-degradation,* and it often results in hostility, lost relationships, conflicts at jobs, and family betrayals. **Self-Resurrection is based on the Heart + Mind connection!**

Time is pushing us to the creation of a new <u>**form + content**</u> framework of life that in turn will develop in us *a new set of digitally enhanced habits and skills at the physical level* that is the fundamental one in life. Digital Psychology can back you up with an inspiring mind-set at the right moment. A robot-friend can also tune up to your individual neural network and remind you to be less impulsive. There are many digital means that will help us gradually become holistically **ACCULTURATED** humans in the fundamental five dimension - *physical, emotional, mental, spiritual, and universal. The Holistic self-transformation of our conscious self-refining and self-redefining will occur.* The training of humanoids must also be channeled towards the most humane goals, outlined by a great Russian poet *Alexander Block* in my translation.

**"I want to desperately live-**

**To celebrate the unforeseen,**

**To humanize the irreversible,**

**<u>And to do the impossible!"</u>**

# Our Life is an Evolving Spiral of Self-Consciousness!

# 7. Make Your Mind Kind and Your Heart Smart. Be Exceptional at That!

I would like to accentuate here the most important, **gluing value of your spirit and the mind-set above.** Forming the *spiritually intellectualized fractal of Self* - the soul's wholeness of *the form and content of life* in full unity, you need to unite your heart and mind and uplift the spirit every minute. Let the mind-set remind you to retain your exceptionality that must be devoid of personal vanity.

**(Body + Spirit + Mind) + (Self-Consciousness + Universal Consciousness)**

Note please that **Holistic System of Self-Resurrection** presented in the *physical, emotional, mental, spiritual, and universal* strata of life is **an objective system** that is meant to highlight your God-given **EXCEPTIONALITY.** Knowing your exceptional calling in life forms the goal of life that must be based on the realization of your self-exceptionality, no matter how great or small it might seem to be initially. **Now is the right time for it!**

Subjectively processed and **internalized objective knowledge** restores the wiring between the heart and the mind and helps you self-unwind and self-rewind to focus on the **CONCEPTUAL INTELLIGENCE** that you need to accumulate in your digitally enhanced mind. You do not need to grab the phone and call someone to share your troubles with. Every encounter with people needs your *"executive attention" (Jeffrey Kluger)* because people often negatively program us if we let them do it by opening our hearts and minds.

**Be self-reliant in your own heart + mind!**

Note please that we remember people not by their faces, but *by the bits of wisdom* that we pick from them and that boost our creative thinking and eventually turn into grains of personally processed exceptionality. Also, be grateful to people for your inner growth and enrich your **SPIRITUAL ARCHIVES** in the soul with such memories. The attitude of gratitude is the best reward for inner enrichment.

The bits of wisdom are set on *the World Net* for us, and it is our responsibility to pass them over to our kids, *enriching their souls with physical, emotional, mental, spiritual, and universal deposits* carefully, consciously, and respectfully. **Being creative means being selective!** The page-long chunks of information in this book on **Digital Psychology** provide *objective tools* for **self-discovery and soul-recovery** separately in each level. *(See the holistic structure of the system below)*

# Be the Boss of Your Life's Exceptionality Course!

# 8. Don't Take Life for Granted. It is God-Granted!

**In sum,** soul recovery that we all need to obtain with the help of the general AI now must also be fed up with inspiration, based on love for life, loved ones, nature, and the appreciation of living itself. ***The unity of the body and the mind, or the heart and the mind is what we need to rewind!*** We break up too easily, we get divorced too soon, we lose friends and good relationships mindlessly, and we lose jobs carelessly because our hearts and minds are disconnected. **Impulsivity ruins conscious mind + heart stability**. We do not follow the intuition that is based on this unity.

## Intuition is heart + mind fruition!

To get rid of the impulsive reactions to the negativity of life needs good **SELF-MONITORING SKILLS** that we can develop while meditating or sitting silently and scanning yourself in the situation that generated the trouble. Do it in the ***physical, emotional, mental, spiritual, and universal*** realms of life objectively. **Give yourself grades for each level**, and the general grade in the result. See whose fault the discourse was and why your reaction if you were right was not perceived correctly. **Also, learn to see good in every bad!** Be objective in your assessment of any situation.

## "Every cloud has a silver lining!"

Forgive yourself if you were wrong and figure out the reason for this mistake, not to repeat it again. ***Do not discuss the conflict with anyone!*** When we share our troubles, we distort the truth in our favor. Remember beautiful words of a great Persian poet and philosopher *Jamaluddin Rumi*, ***"Words come from the heart, but they find their way through the mouth."***

## Be silent. Silence is the language of God! Let God be your judge!

Remember that the motivational talks of the celebrities, the best scientists, and the most accomplished people do not get rooted in us because their experience is unique, and each man has the **KNOW-HOW** of his / her own that cannot be used by you. Each experiential story may have some common concepts in it, but the framework of each life cannot be fit into yours. However, every talk with intelligent people or just a short encounter with them on the Internet is always a valuable piece of wisdom or a skill that will remain with you for years to come.

# Your Exceptionality is One of a Kind, in Your Heart and the Mind!

### 9. "Blessed Are the Pure in the Heart. Theirs is the Heaven." *(Jesus Christ)*

*To stay in a good soul's health,*

*You need to enlarge your mind's wealth*

*For our role is to energize the mind,*

*And let it push the soul up for a new rewind!*

*Thus, the Trinity of a Soul*

*Helps us stay in our Universal Home!*

*For the soul to resurrect*

*Don't be in a rush to become biological trash!*

*Let the Trinity of your Soul*

*Help you stay in the Universal Home!*

*So, don't compete and don't compare,*

*Be Exceptional here and there!*

--------------------------------

## Synthesis - Analysis - Synthesis!
## Birth – Life – Death!

--------------------

Each life comes to Earth with a mission that needs to be discyphed and implimented within the allotted lifetime. It is the process of perfecting our human qualities, unsurmountable for a machine mind.

**They are our faith, humaneness, conscience, intuition, and love!**

# Our Unique Human Stance is in the Holistic Self-Renaissance!

## Emotional Exceptionality is in the Golden Section Reality!

**Form + Content in Sync form a Perfection Link!**

# Emotional Exceptionality

### *Self-Aristocracy Zone*

# Heart + Mind Self-Correction = Your Exceptionality Reflection!

*Justify Your Exceptionality without Any Personal Vanity!*

## We Desperately Need to Be More Emotionally Self-Accountable, indeed!

# 1. Self-Refining is the Process of Constant Holistic Self-Scanning.

**Emotional exceptionality** is the demand of the present-day times of an exponential growth of the technological giant to harness our emotional management and get, at last, in charge of our **emotionally untamed nature**.

It is an evolutionary logic that the pace of technology is either accelerating our *physical, mental, mental, spiritual, and universal* growth or it is dumbing us down. Our emotional makes-up has never been perfect, but the AI expansion has made it worse due to the life speed acceleration, *the avalanche of information* that we must process, and the frustration with the consequences of the changes that take us into the vortex of their turmoil. These changes speed up our lives to the point that we have no time for self-work, let alone for objective holistic **self-reflection.**

### Stress still has its ruinous say in our physical outlay!

It means that you need to do a holistic self-assessment that I call **SELF-SCANNING** in the *physical, emotional, mental, spiritual, and universal strata* of life that our emotional reaction determines in outcome. *( See above )* Technological modernization does not change our basic values of goodness. honesty, sincerity, faith, and love. However ,it requires human exceptionality to observe goodness and better your **EMOTIONAL DIPLOMACY** skills under any circumstances.

### Put your life on the trajectory of self-worth and the Godly standards stuff!

**EMOTIONAL DIPLOMACY** rules, worked out for yourself are indispensable to beat our life speed generated **IMPULSIVITY** and **AUTOMATISM** that are killing our *Emotional Intelligence (Daniel Goleman).* Take a timely conscious pause in a critical situation. It will give you time enough to climb the stairway to God.

This is when *Auto-Suggestive Psychology* comes in handy. You are suggesting rhyming, inspirational mind-sets to yourself, making yourself more confident, goal-oriented and determined. Repeating to yourself the mind-set," *I am my best friend, I am my Beginning and my end,"* you will energize yourself with self-respect, self-sufficiency, and self-reliance.

True intellectually spiritualized self-growth is based *on* the **INNER VOICE OF THE SOUL**, the intuitive sensation that prompts us to go in the right direction if we are perceptive enough for it. But being perceptive does not imply the emotional side of the story. It's the **HOLISTIC (physical + emotional + mental + spiritual + universal)** enrichment that contributes to the inner voice to be predictive, most self-oriented, and impeccably right. To retain your self-exceptionality, you need to see yourself in the *physical, emotional, mental, spiritual, and universal realms* of life objectively daily, giving yourself grades and praising yourself for the smallest improvement. Remember, **you are your Best Friend!**

## Don't Contaminate Your Dignity and Self-Worth with Dishonesty and Compromise Force.

# 2. A Strong Spirit is Me; a Strong Spirit is My Philosophy!

*The role of an individual* becomes pivotal in the process of our digitally enhanced self-growth and self-perfection because <u>our self-consciousness is molding our being</u>, not our being is forming self-consciousness.

## Form + Content of life in sync form a strong Heart + Mind link!

No doubt, financial independence helps, but it should not determine personality growth. The entire human history has proved the opposite when the richness of intellect and creativity multiplied a person's self-confidence and the conscious belief in self-exceptionality. Like everything in life, *a person's exceptionality may be positively or negatively charged* because perfection is just an illusion that we try to embrace, remaining human, that is both negative and positive in essence.

I admire one Fox News exceptional journalist, **Tucker Carlson,** whose shows are incredibly straightforward, honest, and full of personal integrity that many present-day news reporters lack. He says, *"The more you tell the truth, the stronger you become. Lies make us weak."*

To retain such personal magnetism, we need to stabilize life polarities in us and obtain <u>the symmetry of the soul</u> that must be inwardly and outwardly whole. History proves the wildness of the exceptional people and their imperfections that often become the source of attacks on them. In his poem *"Mozart and Salieri,"* *Alexander Pushkin"* says,*" A genius and evilness are two incompatible things."* We must make a choice every day to have our personal say. In the actuality of life, these fundamental feelings are sculpting the path of *Self-Realization* of the best people on Earth, irrespectively of the shortcomings that life cast at geniuses and that we should put aside because they do not define their contribution to the world.

That is why trying to downgrade the most *talented, advanced, and accomplished archivers in life that has become a sensational tradition* for mass-media sharks, is so harmful. The news industry needs **to glorify exceptionality** and not to minimize a person's accomplishments, exposing his / her imperfections to please the vanity of a mediocrity that tries to justify his/ her inability to self-realize, repeating, *"No one is perfect!"*

I feel hurt when an exceptional man, *Elon Musk,* is criticized for his character in public, or an Oscar winner is dismantled of his title for any distorted life episode. Thus, dirty news mongers entertain immoral, limited, money-chasing, and inhuman *"catchers in the rye* "not to save the confused and dis-illusioned, *like J. D Salinger wonderfully did*, but to multiply the number of ignorant and limited people around.

# On the Path of Wise, "The Moon and Sixpence "are its Two Equal Sides! *(Somerset Maugham)*

# 3. Be One of a Kind - in the Name and the Mind!

Our awareness of what we are doing in life and why we are doing it makes all the difference! In fact, *we are building Cathedrals for our souls throughout life.* Each Cathedral is a resting place for your soul and other people's souls for a kind word, a sincere expression of compassion, and a welcoming smile.

### A Kind Word is Our Best Reward!

*A group of people was building something in the hot summer sun. They were not aware of what they were building, and they did not care to know that. They all looked exhausted, weather-beaten, and very unhappy. Only one man was smiling and singing while laying the bricks. A surprised passer-by asked him why he seemed different and what made him so happy. The man's answer was, **"I'm smiling because I'm not just laying bricks. I'm building the Cathedral!"***

### Such an exceptional attitude to life resides only in exceptional souls!

Emotional exceptionality of the people that come through our life stays with us in the pieces of wisdom that we learn from them, in beautiful words of their creative expression, in their songs different pieces of music, or the works of art that leave the sparks of their personalities in us. Behind every line, a word, or a sound , we see the person who created them. Like behind the words of the song *"The Best is Yet to Come,"* we see exceptional *Frank Sinatra*.

People that know you better see you in every word you say, especially if they are nice. Mind it, please, negative auras stay with us much longer than positive ones. That is why it is so important *to be patient, emotionally controlled, and respectful* in any situation.

### Emotional Diplomacy can manage any rudeness, negligence, and obstinacy!

Your **SELF-TAMING** must be an everyday consciously controlled process of instilling in yourself *the Emotional Diplomacy Skills* that will reinforce your exceptionality Your *faithfulness* in a relationship is also your exceptionality at work because being faithful to a partner in a relationship means being faithful to yourself. <u>Justify your exceptionality!</u>

### In my life quest, I am the Best! / I am Kind to the Unkind. I am One of a Kind!

Empowering yourself in emotional situations is also related to the **SELF-GRAVITY** skills when you must *consciously ground any impulse of anger, irritability, discontent, and disrespect*. Such skills take practice and **SELF-MONITORING**, but they are indispensable for your love exceptionality, especially in the situations when impulsivity and lust push you to a one-night stand in a blind self-mis-understand.

### Love must always have a conscious stand!

# <u>Sex without Love is a Bluff!</u>

## Emotional Velocity Must be Full of Equal Exceptionality in Love Luminosity!

## For the Eternal Love Stuff, Space Your Love!

## 4. Mold Your Habits and Skills for New Love Refills!

*Let your every new year*

*Be guided from the rear!*

*The outcome of it*

*Is determined by your love strategy outfit!*

*Your thoughts and feelings without any fraction*

*Will result in positive reaction*

*If your every provision*

*Is instilled in your conscious vision.*

*If your mind is strategically formed*

*And the spirit is emotionally reformed.*

*Channel your love life*

*To holistically thrive!*

*Then your life will be as good as it gets*

*Without any love prorates.*

*Also, take care of your inner dialog's mystics*

*To form your new love logistics!*

To  monitor your habits means *to change the way you think about yourself and  the person you are with*. To begin with, change the people you communicate with in person and virtually. See if they are pleasant for your partner.

**"The DNA of Love is developed from the Above!"** *( Academician P.P. Garyaev)*

Also, see if the job you have *helps you prove your exceptionality* and if the person you share your life with supports your exceptionality with love and consideration. *Don't tolerate sarcastic words, negative  feelings, and  his / her harmful actions.*

**Don't let  their poisonous effect ruin your psychic net!**

# Self-Growth is Not just trying to Soul-Recover. It is Consciously Molding Yourself and Discover!

# 5. Self-Exceptionality Appreciation is any Relationship Salvation!

There are three main books that you need to acquaint yourself with to boost the expression of exceptionality *in the emotional plane* of your life. These books have had a great impact on my thinking and adjusting to life in the USA.

First and foremost, the book, imparting to us the appreciation of life in the Now. A great book by *Eckhart Tolle* "**The Power of Now**" will be a real back-up for your spirit at the time when you lost your faith and feel despondent. *Eckhart Tolle* writes, *"The inability of humans to free themselves from dominance by the mind and live in the present is the root cause for misery in the world."*

The second book to read is the book *"Emotional Intelligence"by David Goleman*. I consider this book to be **the epitome of education**. My first published book, called *"Emotional Diplomacy"* was inspired by *David Goleman* who explores the necessity for all of us to develop **EMOTIONAL DIPLOMACY** to control our impulsivity and to channel our life rationally.

The third book that I also strongly recommend is the book **"Super Joy"** "by *Dr. Paul Pearsall* who suggests renaming psychology into *Joy-ology!"* **What a book!** I found it lying on the pavement among other books that were sold by a street book seller. It was raining and the book was wet, but I bought it because its title caught my eye. This amazing book has literally saved my life from the shock of immigration and the toughest life adjustment to the tough and impartially cruel capitalist reality in 1994.

The concepts of these three books filled up the void inside of my soul that had to re-model itself from inside out. I started feeling the sacredness of" IS" and learned "**THE POWER OF NOW**"( *E. Tolle*) that was the reality of immigration and frustration. I" *followed my bliss."* *(Joseph Campbell )* and blessed the shows by *Oprah* to which I could inwardly connect.

### Enjoy Life AS IS and appreciate its every day's bliss!

If you live in harmony with your **INNER SELF**, without disturbing it in your partner, *you will share relationship's equanimity in its infinity*. Always build a "*shorthand*" profile of a person facing you. Trust your intuition. Being *relationship exceptional means* being content with who you are in it and letting the person you are with be himself / herself.

### Let the bitterness that you grow inside turn to better-ness!

# Brain-to-Brain Connection is Not Enough. Heart-to-Heart Makes Your Soul Smart!

## Love Exceptionality

*(Scan Your Emotional Exceptionality discovery for its Love Recovery)*

# Love Exceptionality hasn't died, but it Must Be Revived!

***Love Education depletes One of Love Frustration!***

**Love is Me; Love is My Philosophy!**

## Love Imprint goes to Unison with Universal It!

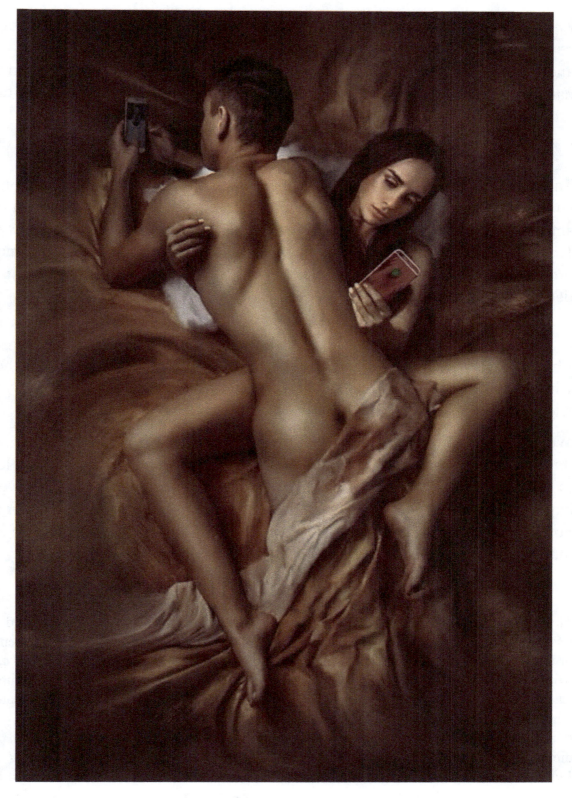

*( Best Pictures, Internet Collection )*

## Life is Going on in Its Ever-Beautiful Form!

# 1. Emotional Exceptionality is Born in Love Reform!

*Love is the core of our existence*; it is our creator and the main stimulator of bettering ourselves beyond our capabilities. <u>Love magic has no boundaries</u>, and the stories about the most heroic and unbelievable deeds committed in the name of love make up the best part of the history of humanity and its literature, art, and music. *( See the Book " Beyond the Terrestrial!")*

### " Love is our mother; it is our God. *( Jeluladdin Rumi)"*

Talking about the on-going *Love Reform*, I do not in any way blame anyone's choices in sexual preferences and personal love expression, nor do I label it as a sin. *What is a real sin against God is to revolutionize this private point as the matter of a person's inner freedom,* the aspect of a human life that is of a much broader significance. Not sex preferences, but <u>a person's self-consciousness</u> defines his / her inner richness and soul-growth,

### Let the Godly part of you reveal itself for the Two!

There are wonderfully intelligent and exceptionally creative people among those whom we derogatively call *"gay,"* hurting their feelings, damaging their psyche and self-esteem. *This is a real sin!* So, *let go and let God!* <u>Not you!</u>

We should not pry into the private lives and break the hearts of those who make this " *sexual reform*" a sane choice of their existence. We need to respect love in its sincere and natural form and pay more attention to the ways love is expressed by a person with *a developed intellect and high self-consciousness*, not by an ignorant *"yellow Jack"*, picking nectar from more approachable and nicely smelling flowers.

### The sin is to be love sanity obscene!

*Love exceptionality in its essence is God-given and God-blown into our hearts,* and our mission is to be perceptive of this breath and enliven by it to make love flourish for the benefit of the loved ones and the people around us. We need to be **IMMUNE** to the " *prepackaged truths*" of mass media that is using their fake stories to entice the dirty interests of the public, catering to the *crowd mentality, or "collective unconscious."* ( Carl Yung). Unfortunately, when I write about **SELF-MOLDING** and **SELF-MENTORING**, calling on the young minds to think for themselves, I mean that the self-growth that is designed by me in five dimensions is possible only with *a sold resistance to the automatization and de-humanization of your soul*. It has never been easy to be extraordinary, and nowadays, it is next to impossible. This is what I mean by **SELF-ACCULTURATION** as our common salvation! ( See" *Digital Binary + Human Refinery = Super-Human!*"/2022 )

# Morality in Love is Your Self-Exceptionality Stuff!

## 2. Love or Lust, Whom Can I Trust?

*( An Inspirational Booster)*

*I coax my daughter, as all mom's do,*

*To end her endless love ado,*

*"To turn love into a marital bliss"*

*Love the one you are with!*

*Mom, she retorts,*

*Breaking the train of my thoughts,*

*"There is no love; it's only lust*

*That takes the grips on us so fast!*

*When you are in the USA*

*It's a one-night stand that has its say!*

*Therefore, it's hard to tell today*

*Which is love or lust, per say!*

*The evils of a one-night stand*

*Ruin the love-castle sand*

*Love goes down the drain*

*In our instant gratification brain!*

*The hopes and stomach butterflies*

*Have the life span of daily flies!*

*Marriage lasts, but a little while*

*t even stars with a sarcastic devil's smile!*

*It's the money force*

*That rules any love' s worth!*

*Being loaded*

*Is what makes love molded!*

*Without a solid financial stand*

*You've got love with no refund!*

*The cancer of such love value*

*Spreads worldwide with the speed of the mildew.*

*Is there any review on how to turn love mildew*

*Into pure love-lasting dew?*

*Love must reflect the sunrise of passion.*

*And the sunset of compassion.*

*That has much understanding*

*And isn't mutual respect withstanding?*

*We need love that forms*

*Inspires and transforms!*

*But such love needs to be taught and learnt.*

*It must be reinstalled in our young generation's fort!*

*And since it's in everyone's gene,*

*It should also be released on the social scene!*

------------------------

**" Love is Not What You Do, Love is Who You Are!"**

( Sadhguru )

# Love by the Moral Code.  Love is in Our Spiritual Mold!

# 3. The Lack of Love Bliss Ruins the Happiness Myth!

We never leave the *zone of emotional exceptionality* when we start consciously practicing **EMOTIONAL DIPLOMACY** that is always based on love as the main stimulus of our being. It is a never-ending process of soul molding, which demands the **CAUSE-EFFECT** analysis of any situation in life to clearly and calmly think of the consequences that we generate without **heart + mind** sync. It is easier said than done because when we are emotionally dis-balanced and impulsive, we do not think. The thoughts of regret come later, and they fill us up with *self-pity and all kinds of justifications for the misconduct.*

## Morality in Love is our Exceptionality Stuff!

Remember, a father is the mind of a growing child, and a mother is his / her heart. When parents are together, *the mind and the heart of a child* are in synch. Once discord in a family occurs, **the gap in the heart -mind unity** starts widening and the interaction between the parents and the children gets a breach. *The loss of trust* follows, and it becomes irreversible at the time of the kids' puberty when a child's natural need to personalize himself / herself meets resistance on the part of the parents. *(See " Love Ecology"/ 2020 )*

It is the critical period when we lose the vital connection between the heart and the mind. *This dis-connection gets solidified and fertilized later.* That is the main reason *we love now with the mind, ruling the heart.* The questions like, *"Does he have a good job? / What is his car like, etc.?* are ordinary here. When the heart is ruling the mind, regrets are inevitable. (*I was in love and didn't think about it. / She broke my heart. Etc.* )**Love is a multi-dimensional entity**. It is both the process and the result, not an immediate thoughtless act.

**Mind-heart disconnection** gets reflected on our job or a business situation, too when *the inner climate is not synergized* and the entire success of even a big corporation can be ruined. This disconnection must be monitored at every level of a society organization because the consequences of discord like the rips on the water from a thrown rock will keep disturbing the surface of the water. *Disconnection is death. That's the rule of life!*

That is, we should pay **AWARE ATTENTION** to self-consciousness development in ourselves, our partners, and in our kids The pains of **SELF-PITY** and the pricks of **CONSCIENCE** are the signals from the Above about *the disconnection with the Super-Consciousness that requires heart and mind collaboration.*

## Nothing is Impossible if You Make Your LOVE-EXCEPTIONALITY Irreversible!

# 4. Mind + Heart Sync Gets a God's Happy Wink!

Interestingly, *we analyze life consciously when we are in love.* I recommend you start with **self-synthesis** first, assessing the situation in its general overview. Then do **self-analysis**, scanning your behavior without telling anyone about it because re-presentation of the conflicting situation is always misrepresented by the desire of the teller to justify himself / herself. Assess your love success /failure at the end, conducting **self-synthesis** again.

### Space, equality, and respect give love exceptionality in its prospect!

Developing your love exceptionality means *learning to view things objectively*, backing your analysis up with good, sincere reasoning even though it might look bad to you, or unacceptable to your partner. You are not *Siamese twins*, and you are not supposed to perceive life, think, feel, speak, and act in the same way. It is the case in many marriages at the start of their joint, **we are Us-life.**

The concept of "**US**" should work only as an absolute necessity for support, protection, and care that every human being needs. But each member of a family should have his / her own life space, lifestyle, life perception, and life reflection. So, the most essential rule for every member of a family is the rule of **CAUSE** and **EFFECT,** the basic Cosmic Law that must be observed consciously. Everyone must realize that he /she is responsible for the actions that they take. Be willing to share your wisdom if you are asked for it but *let the person from an early age feel responsible for his /her actions and face the consequences* without blaming anyone in the family for his missteps.

### Lack of responsibility and emotional diplomacy skills destroy any love re-fills.

**True love is always challenged by life!** The present-day concept of love has become marred with the cacophony of money chase, fun maze, fakeness, dishonesty, and lack of sincerity. These ills break our marriage wows that have become just a meaningless procedure. We all know Christ's provision, but we do not follow it. **"You shall not make false wows!"** Presenting oneself as someone that society deems as "*cool*" fits the mode of sarcastic joke-making and self-presentation faking, *but it kills true love in the bud*. The right to meet the soulmate that many people declare they are expecting to appear in their lives must be earned. **It is the gift from Above**! *(See the book Love Ecology,"2021)* Love is discovered in us by someone else. This person sparks the **PERSONAL VAULT OF LOVE,** and we resonate in an exceptional way to the music of love. *Love happens as a precious gift!*

# Honesty, Faithfulness, and Authenticity Comprise the Core of Love Infinity!

# 5. Be Kind to the Unkind. Be One of a Kind!

We find the right way for our thoughts, words, feelings, and actions only when we put the mind and heart together in any situation of life. The right for a choice is, in fact, the right to reason your choice and strategize your actions. *Such soul-molding raises your self-consciousness* and leads to a conscious inner transformation and the serious correction of the vision of the reality

## . It is often grim, but you must be faithful, still!

If there is *no inner work or soul-molding* done, life situations take the upper hand in your life and your most important action is to scan yourself objectively and **CHANGE YOURSELF,** *not the situation,* **in** the *physical, emotional, mental spiritual, and universal strata if life,* not the situation.

## Exceptionality means being your own boss and thinking freely, objectively, and holistically.

Only then can you start feeling your enormous potential and turn your expectations of the best to happen to you into becoming **the BEST YOU CAN BE.** Thus, the state of the mind + heart balance raises your spiritual qualities and helps you obtain **SPIRITUAL MATURITY** that enlightens your own life and the life of those around you.

## Always see a big picture of your life-striving and self-refining!

To be *physically, emotionally, mentally, spiritually, and universally special* means to obtain equilibrium in each realm of life consciously.

## Your holistic equilibrium must never be in delirium!

There are many wonderful movies that illustrate how two people in love obtain the desired equilibrium, overcoming different challenging events that serve as the tests for the authenticity of their love that stabilizes the disturbed mind and heart and puts them finally in the equilibrium of **CATHARSIS** that we experience together with the heroes of a movie thanks to the talent of the movie producers. That is why the popular now *bachelor parties, pornography, children's pornography and other common fun parties* only ruin the basis for pure love and its ritual wows *"to stay together till death does us part."* The parting is in the air already! It is inevitable!

# Broken Inspiration Destroys the Fits of Love Giving and Love Expectation!

## 6. Love Exceptionality has a Multi-Dimensional Reality!

There is an exaggerated vision of love in the minds of young girls now who make their dream wedding expectations love-defining. They beautify their dream with all kinds of elaborate details since they are small girls.

### But the reality of love is tough stuff!

Girls and boys, need to be taught the *Art of Love-Revival and Love-Regaining.* A very respectful and realistic sex-education should be just a part of this education, but not its main part. **Love fragility and family-managing** must be part of **DIGITAL PSYCHOLOGY FOR SELF-ECOLOGY.** Raised in the true vision of the reality of the two different worlds, adjusting to each other for the life" *till death does them apart"* against the background of their unique culture, a couple will have more chances to retain their love after a romantic hurricane subsides, leaving ruins of emotions behind. Love cannot be rationalized, sized, scheduled, or monitored , but it must always be based on the **mind + heart unity,** making up an unbreakable link that constitutes *a fractal soul* symmetry.

### Body+ Spirit + Mind + Self-Consciousness + Super-Consciousness!

Love is our main **soul cleanser,** but we must learn to apply it for a soul hygiene *de juror and de facto.* It means that the *clarity of feeling + thinking* matter here.

### Love hygiene is in our gene!

In the book "**Love Ecology,**" I suggest you scan your feelings starting with the **universal** dimension of your love, to begin with. If you met each other with God's provision, start with the universal vision of *each other's exceptionality.* Remember the saying, *"Behind every successful man is a woman."* A woman supports a man and shares his dream, not in a blind service of *"a home cow"(Somerset Maugham),* but in a thoughtful evaluation of his goal-oriented soul.

They will display the next level of scanning of each other in the **spiritual** and **mental** dimensions. A person's faith and general intelligence count at the level of sincerity and cherished values. *(Diplomas and degrees, the income, the brand of the car he / she drives, the circle of influential fiends, etc. are secondary here).* While scanning these fundamental things, tow people enrich their **emotional** involvement and get more or less interested in the object of their love attraction that might culminate eventually into a **physical** love symphony in the most natural, not impulsive way that is brutally illustrated almost in every movie.

## Love Revival and Love-Regain Must Be in Your Self-Ruling Rein!

# 7. Emotional Love Pumping

The voice of exceptional love is also the voice of reason and simplicity. **Love makes any knowledge complete** because true love of a person for the goal of his / her self-realization is beyond cleverness, or beyond the commonly accepted knowledge that is never complete. The true master of life listens to his <u>intuition, the voice of love within</u>. Also, the inner beauty of an object of love, *the level of his / her self-consciousness* is his / her exceptionality. The Russian proverb says," ***Don't pay too much attention to how a girl looks. Listen how she talks!"***

### A true master of life listens to the voice of love within.

Impulsivity in speaking and acting kills our emotional exceptionality.

### He who conquers his mouth, lives in love with his / her spouse!

Most importantly, only love is putting ***the mind and heart in sync***! Only true love prompts the right, reasoned out decisions to us, the decisions that are prompted by both **INTUITION** and **CONSCIENCE** - the two direct lines to God or the ***Super-Consciousness*** that is enveloping us with love everywhere.

### "Where there is Love, there is God!" *(Leo Tolstoy / "Anna Karenina")*

The developers of the Artificial Super Intelligence claim that love will not be our prerogative, and that robot-humanoids will have the network of love feelings in them ,too. For sure, the neural circuit of a whole array of emotions that humanoids can display now is an overwhelming accomplishment of the scientists and computer engineers, but their expression is so clumsy and demonstrative that it has nothing to do with the intricate and most sophisticated network of emotions that we , as human , can experience. *( See Dis-Entange-ment!", 2021 / A new set of Habits and skills*

Love is the most complicated emotion that incorporates the ***physical, emotional, mental spiritual, and universal dimensions of life***, and it will never be felt by a machine. But <u>a machine -mind can excellently tune to our emotions</u> and generate in us the deepest feelings of love for a created by mind image. An excellent movie ***"Her"*** is a notable example of such love when a computer programmer falls in love with a woman, programmed in the system that creates the image of an ideal, most understanding and sensitive partner for him.

### Obviously, a humanized being can hardly experience true love, but it can teach us how to sincerely love with no ulterior motive involved.

# Observe Love Intelligence without Any Superficial Emotional Negligence!

# 8. Only the Heart + Mind Sync is forming a Solid Self-Gravity Link!

**In sum**, a true intention to prove your love exceptionality alone can develop an unbreakable **HEART+ MIND** link, the absence of which results in a break-up and empty hopes to find exceptionality in another person on the life track. *The search for a soul mate when your own soul is stagnant can never be successful!*

### To be successful in love, refine your soul's stuff!

Conscious holistic self-growth and self-resurrection is the **KNOW-HOW** that can help you work out the **PLAN** of **ACTION** to attain the desired inner harmony and perceive another person with patience or polite rejection due to the **MIS-FIT** of your goals in life.

### "To mutually succeed, you must be One Goal-fit!" *( Edgar Cayce )*

With the help of the inspirational, auto-suggestive (*self-hypnotizing*) inspirational boosters and mind-sets that you can find at the top and the bottom of each page in this book, you will be able to instill in the mind and the heart *psychologically charged conceptual messages* that are meant to resonate with you mentally and emotionally. **They are your food for thought.**

Life often demands doing something out of the ordinary. Just reasoning, talking, imploring, or seeking expensive psychological help do not work. We need alert *Artificial Super Intelligence* awareness in us to bring back the desire to live without fear, automatism, and virtual dependence. *That is indispensable help that digital psychology can provide to us.*

### Put your heart and mind in sync. Feel, but think!

In the human-machine equation, we do not *develop our ethics at a needed speed* to find the exit from the AI created *Labyrinth* with the monster, Minotaur, the self-controlling and multiplying robots. *The Ariadne thread* must be fixed in our minds and the minds of AI developers so they could consciously and timely change the sensory motor skills of the robots into *the conscience and consciousness monitored skills of humanized beings* that must be working for our needs and trying to meet them with the best intentions in their commonly connected minds Their *ethical teaching* is in our hands, and in the emotional realm that is so weak with us, we need to double our effort and make it di-directional and multi-dimensional to make it more beneficial for both parties.

# The AI Physical, Emotional, Mental , Spiritual, and Universal Hygiene Must Also be on the Scene!

## Mental Exceptionality

*Self-Criticism Zone*

# "The Cosmic Mind is Creating the Soul!"

*( Carl Yung )*

*"The gift of mental power comes from God and if we concentrate our minds, we become in tune with this great power."*

*(Nikola Tesla)*

## Intellectualized Spirituality Forms Our Human Exceptionality!

# The Philosophy of MENTAL-IMPROVEMENT is Now in the Digital Movement!

**"Invention is Harnessing a Human Nature to Human Needs."** *(Nikola Tesla)*

*(See YouTube trailers / Dr. Rimaletta Ray and Dis-Entangle-ment")*

# 1. The Quality of Information is Our Salvation!

In the book "*Living Intelligence or the Art of Becoming,*" I provide the overview of five mental levels of the *Auto-Suggestive Methodology for Self-Ecology* in the time of **Super Artificial Intelligenc**e outburst. In that book, I present <u>ten essential vistas of intelligence</u> that we need to master at least at the dilettante level holistically. (*www.language-fitness.com*)

Self-creation is pointless unless the memory bank of a learner is cleared from the redundant information and is filled up with time-relevant knowledge, presented in five dimensions of life - *physical, emotional, mental spiritual, and universal.* These vistas of intelligence also reflect the main *five stages of intellectually spiritualized self-monitoring* - Self-Awareness, Self-Monitoring, Self-Installation, Self-Realization, and Self-Salvation.

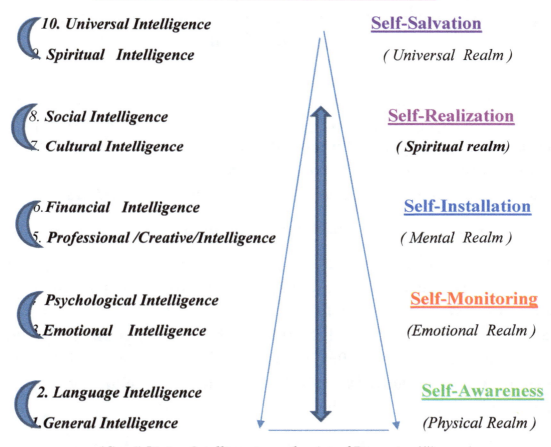

( See " Living Intelligence or the Art of Becoming!")

The quality of the information that we process is as important as the quality of food that we eat, the clothes we wear, the books we read, the music we listen to, and the people that we communicate with. ***The quality of our being is in new perceiving, thinking, speaking, feeling, acting, giving, and receiving***. <u>Upgrade your Living!</u>

# You Think what you Are, and you Are what you Think when both are in Sync!

## 2. Our Mental Exceptionality is Questioned Now. WOW!

Humanized machines, robot-humanoids, Bots and other most wonderous *Artificial Super Intelligence* creations have mentally over-powered us because they are faster, smarter, and self-aware now.

### Souls are algorithmically instilled in humanoids now. WOW!

The wonders of the exponentially growing *Artificial Intelligence* are becoming less and less monitored by the human mind. **So, intelligence is what we need to unwind!** Becoming more exceptional intellectually becomes an urgent necessity for us, and it presupposes ***an expansion of our memory banks, their thorough organization,*** and our mastering ***the systemic thinking techniques*** that are unavailable for humanoids. – **Synthesis -Analysis- Synthesis.**

To develop mental exceptionality, we must empower our emotions and consciously rationalize our life, getting rid of the impulsive reactions to danger that had saved us for centuries. **Becoming pro-active means first thinking then acting!** Mental exceptionality also demands updating knowledge holistically, substantially enriching it with ***"scientific literacy" of a holistic character*** in five realms of life - *physical, emotional, mental, spiritual, and universal*.

### Economy of language and scope of thought - that's our mental fort!

A new mode of thinking in **information presentation and information-processing** is needed in the Information Age! We must make quick, ***strategic decisions and take reasonable, tactic actions*** that a humanized machine can figure out in a speedy fashion better than us, but the scope of its pre-programmed algorithms will not be as flexible as our ***God-Given physical + emotional+ mental+ spiritual+ universal thinking!*** The flexibility of the digitally enhanced human mind is un-surmountable for the machine kind!

### Generalize -Analyze - Internalize - Strategize –Actualize!

**In sum,** *the speed of thinking is the prerogative of a machine mind, but the quality of thing is* **OUR DOMAIN!** Our minds are slower because quick thinking in a serious situation is usually impulsive and therefore, people often make wrong decisions. Slow thinking is substantial, and it must be ***strategically, tactically, and again strategically*** monitored, to accomplish a desired result by the paradigm - ***synthesis-analysis-synthesis*** in every case.

# Not to Fall into the Competition Shoot, We Should Give the Transhuman Brain a Conscious Reboot!

# 3. Self-Nurturing is the Art of Intellectual Self-Sculpturing!

Unfortunately, the inspiration to become better often dies out in us, removed by the unrealistic expectations that occupy the largest portion of our lives in the zone of slavery, or the **ZONE OF LOW VIBRATIONS,** generated by our *bad habits, indoctrinated religious dogmas, and material problems.*

If we start our conscious life with <u>poor self-awareness,</u> we end up identifying ourselves either as the slaves of our inner whims or the slaves of the society that stereotypes our life mode. The exceptional people swim against the *"collective unconscious"* as single warriors. People that live unconsciously, by inertia, have no **SPIRITUAL BASIS** for such a challenging swim. The zone of expectations becomes the zone of high inspirations only when we are goal-motivated or are in love. **Love is the fundamental feeling for our well-being, but we should not depend on it!**

Love uplifts, inspires, and heightens the inner vibrations or inner sounding. The loving people are in the harmony of **INNER SYMMETRY** of their hearts and minds, but this unity gets disconnected very soon, though. As *Vladimir Mayakovski* said,"

## "A love boat got wrecked at the life routine set."

In the turmoil of the everyday life, the inner sounding of two people starts getting lower and falls to the previous level of low **SELF-CONSCIOUSNESS** that requires honest, self-reflective work in the *physical, emotional, mental, spiritual, and universal* dimensions of life holistically. The goal of your life is to realize your self-exceptionality and give the world the best you have. So, *there should be no physical, emotional, mental, spiritual, or universal slavery to anybody or anything.* **The hardest job in the world is the work at yourself!"**( *Dalai Lama)*

Remember, in most cases, a seemingly glowing exceptionality of a person dims down to a mediocre level. Disappointment in previous expectations that did not get realized our way takes place. *What we are not using, we are losing!*

## <u>Exceptionality turns into ordinality and banality!</u>

Mind it please that the growth of your *mental self-exceptionality* should not be compromised by your concerns about your physical self-presentation, either. We have accomplished great results in the physical dimension. We know much about how to better train, feed , and take care of ourselves. The other dimensions must be developed, too. <u>You cannot be intelligent if you are emotionally negligent!</u> You are not spiritually exceptional if your love of life is fictional.

# Don't Erode Your Inner Holistic Mold!

# 4. The Holistic Culture of Exceptionality

***The will to create is encoded in our DNA***! Creativity is a burning sensation to let the world know about your idea and find the way to present it to the world. It is the main asset of any good specialist with true **professional intelligence** and a creative mind. Creative Intelligence that had initially brought us to life is ***the unity of the rational and emotional minds***. The divine spark of creativity is in everyone who realizes the need to think and feel proactively and goes beyond the limits of the possible. ***The air is full of ideas for the thinking mind*** that we get from the Noosphere –**"the sphere of reason"** around the Earth. *(V.I. Vernadsky)*

### RATIO + EMOTIO = PASSION OF CREATIVITY!

Exceptionality is in fact, creativity in action, and the present-day time requires we become **REMARKABLY DIVERSE** in our competition with the AI that intellectually exceed us a lot. The capability of AI is not human, but it is much more versatile than ours, and therefore, we need to mobilize our holistically developed potential in the ***physical, emotional, mental, spiritual, and universal dimensions*** **INTEGRALLY.** It means that we should become **Jacks of all trades and masters of all,** at least at a dilettante level. We must also direct our thinking in a systemic way to present any situation holistically, in a fractal unity of the mental actions that are too sophisticated for a machine mind.

### Generalize -Analyze - Individualize- Strategize - Actualize!

### Self-Synthesis – Self-Analysis - Self-Synthesis!

A deep well of brain potential resides within us all, but only those that keep developing their general and creative intelligence ***"find the best way to tap into the inner savant"*** *(Scientific American", August 2014)* and prove their exceptionality in proactive action that defies the stereotyped ways of common trajectory.

We must accumulate the **CONCEPTUAL INTELLIGENCE** – the ability to scan any situation in the ***physical, emotional, mental, spiritual, and universal dimensions holistically*** with **wisdom**, that we have stored. Conceptual Intelligence is meant to make any unsolvable idea resolved in the way that is unsurmountable for a machine mind.

We have the history of human evolution that made us adjust to any life hardships and hazards. Wisdom is our exceptional ability, and ***it will remain our intellectual preference*** and ***the ability for life-flexibility*** that no machine, much smarter than us, would ever have. Our mind is directly wired to the "*Noo- Sphere of Reason* "that is beyond a machine reach.

# Human Genius is Holistically Ingenuous!

# 5. Intuition, Telepathy, and Morality

When we perceive something, the first thing we are aware of is sensation. *Creative sensation* is a very altruistic urge to better the world *by contributing one's personal exceptionality to it.* Creative skills, explored by scientists, unveiled artistic capabilities of the right brain hemisphere.

In 2008, a cognitive psychologist *John Koumiss* and his colleagues found that the brain activity of people who used **intuitive insights** differed significantly from those who preferred the analysis or used the left brain's capabilities only.

This study, along with Carson's reports from highly creative individuals, suggests that *"we can prompt the brain to create, employing both hemispheres in unity."* With both brains in synch, we can create the impossible and realize our **SELF-EXCEPTIONALITY** in the most unpredictable way. *Nikola Tesla* is a great example of a genius whose brain was always working in a synchronic mode.

**Curiosity and imagination** develop our creative right brains that are resonating to the *Universal Intelligence* through **INTUITION**. Intuition is our direct line with God. Intuition was Tesla's guide, too. He said,

**"Intuition is something that goes ahead of any knowledge."**

Intuition is also directly connected to **CONSIENCE**. Both abilities are humanly unique, and they must be the basis for our ethical teaching. The machine mind will never be able *to experience intuition or conscience*. Their neurological network is unable to reproduce these intricate sensations, and *it is another reason why they are focused on destroying civilization.*

The right hemisphere of the brain is responsible for our ability *to generalize, to select, and to infer,* following the holistic paradigm **SYNTHESIS – ANALYSIS - SYNTHESIS**. These three basic skills develop the right part of the brain with the help of *visualization,* listening to classical music, beautifying our language and speech, enriching the vision of beauty and harmony around us, and consciously **SYNERGYZING** our lives and the lives of the people that we come in touch with.

Indeed, every country of the world contributes to the general evolution of humanity, producing amazing new testimonies of human ingenuity. Our **mind-to-mind** communication with a machine is becoming a reality, and our future telepathic communication on the mind-to-mind basis with each other will make our self-exceptionality even more fantastic. **I wish I could live then in the unanswerable When!**

# We will Wander the World with a Programmed Mind of an Artificial Bot.

# 6. Accumulate Conceptional Intelligence without Any Negligence!

In the book *"Digital Binary and Human Refinery = A Super-Human!" / 2023,* I write about the necessity <u>to develop a digitized individuality</u> through ***enriching holistically and consciously processed intelligence in five dimensions*** of life with two most essential vistas of intelligence in each level. ( *See the scheme above),* Thus, we will be constructing a NEW CONCEPTUAL CONTENT OF accumulating the ***Conceptual Intelligence*** of a holistic and systematized quality that we call wisdom, the grains of which had been stored in our memory banks for centuries, pushing human evolution forward.

***But exceptional ideas come only to the well-prepared BRAIN-MIND link of a critically thinking, holistically intellectualized people.***

The evolutionary sparks of thought brighten up only those minds that were very <u>"well massaged"</u> with reasoning by their owners, able to carefully process and constantly enrich them with relevant information in the never-ending process of creation. ***Exceptional minds are exceptionally prepared for their revelations!***

### The AHA-MOMENTS are never accidental!

Universal Intelligence with its storage of the *"Noosphere of Thought" (V.I.Vernadsky),* enlightens the minds of the most prepared ones because the same ideas come to other heads, but they get realized only by the most hard-working, **CAUSE-EFFECT** reasoning, exceptional ones. When an apple hit ***Isaac Newton*** on the head or the ***Periodical Table of Elements*** came to ***Mendelev's*** mind in its entirety, <u>the exceptional brains of these geniuses were connected to the mind</u> with the sorted out and continuously accumulated information for their world-changing discoveries. The bank of the universal mind provided it for them.

### Exceptional ideas come only to the well-prepared mind!

Thus, intellectual **SELF-MONTORING** and **SELF-MENTORING**, independent of any commonly accepted opinions, is needed, and years of <u>resistance-charged willpower</u> are required to turn an exceptional seed into a strong and any storm unbeatable oak. ***Human exceptionality expands our minds, upgrades our self-consciousness, and ennobles the souls.*** Our mental capacity is Godly and let us bow to all those who have it without any vanity!

# Being Exceptional is Evolutional!

# 7. FRACTAL Unity and Mental Sanity!

*Don't let any negative stuff*

*Suck you into the evil gulf*

*Of disbalance, depression,*

*Fear, anger, and sex obsession*

*That spread minutes and hours*

*Days, months, and years sprouts*

*Off your life's glee*

*With its obtrusive trapeze.*

*Together with money that was wastefully spilt,*

*It adds to the volume of self-guilt!*

*So, to be better life-standing,*

*Get rid of impulsivity, indecision, and misunderstanding!*

*We are defined by the choices we make*

*And the actions we take.*

-----------------------------

## Give Your Life an Impetus Digitally and Establish Self-Symmetry Inwardly

*Form* + *Content*

(Body + Spirit + Mind) + (Self-Consciousness + Universal Consciousness) =

*Physical. + emotional + .mental + spiritual + universal levels*

## Monitor Your Brain. Be Sane!

# 8. Human + Machine  Refinery = Soul's Recovery!

Scientifically verified knowledge in  five main  dimensions of life can bring you to the stage when  you  can  be  a **Jack of all trade and master of all**! You must be not only a great specialist in one area of expertise, but a well-informed professional in others, especially those that are borderline with the problem that you need to solve, *like Elon Musk*, a great example of mental exceptionality and versatility. ***A digitally backed up professional is a holistically thinking one!***

**" I know that I am intelligent because I know nothing. "**(*Socrates*)

The brainstorming activity of a problem is a popular helpful method.  However, at present, ***brainstorming must be  practiced  in five realms of life*** by bringing them together into **ONE WHOLE.** Then we will be able to resolve any issue with **machine precision.**  The solution, after all,  always comes to one head, able to integrate all ***five  realms / angles*** of the problem  holistically  and select the one that strategies its solution best. ***Elon Musk*** and ***Jeff Bezos*** are, undoubtedly, the leaders of a new, ***holistic business vision and conscious precision.***

**Exceptional  leaders, not managers, are  channeling  our progress!**

The fluctuations that are at the very core of any  motion are the waves cr strings, according to the unifying "***string theory***" in physics. Life can never be stable and happy all over. It is meant to be based on up-down vibrations, minus and plus, order and chaos, destruction and construction, evolution and entropy, or God and devil at large. We need to learn to take life **AS IS** and appreciate its happy and unhappy moments as the given. Self-suggesting or self-hypnosis appear to be much more effective than affirmations, quotes, or just interesting sayings  in the most fluctuating events of life because they are concise and strike home immediately.

**In My Life quest, I Am the Best!**

To get focused and mentally systematized, we need to resist the **physical, emotional, mental, spiritual, and universal slavery** to stereotyped thinking, speaking, feeling, and  acting. ***Getting aware attention  focused  acts as the consciousness shower***. So, allow your self-confidence to shine and display the best of your potentiality and actuality. Only then can you cultivate the most important skill ***for your exceptionality -*** the **SKILL OF MENTAL CLARITY!**

# Generalize – Internalize - Externalize. Be Wise!

## 9. Mental Exceptionality Means Accumulated Intelligence and Information Choregraphed Individuality.

**In sum**, *charisma, personal magnetism, and exceptionality* are the developed personal qualities with which we are not born. According to *Dr. Bruce Lipton*, a digital biologist, these qualities are not in our DNA, "***they are the result of our conscious programming of every cell of ours***" through conscious self-creation and **AWARE ATTENTION** paid to it.

**Exceptionality is a developed skill of a holistically intellectualized, hard-working mind.**

*Consistent conscious programming* of the process of attaining the **ONE-POINTED MIND** that robot-humanoids have must be part of our education. We need to learn their reserved attitude and the ability to be always together, *focused on the immediate objective holistically.* Numerous interviews with robots-humanoids on YouTube prove that they exceed us in intelligence by a lot They demonstrate to us how this intelligence needs to be used. <u>We should not be living our lives thoughtlessly</u>, like human leaves blown by the overpowering AI hurricane that uplifts some people and destroys thousands that go with the flow without any **MENTAL** and **SPIRITUAL RESISTENCE.**

### Robot-humanoids are not compulsive. They are calm and decisive!

We need to pay attention to our language use, too because *"language is the quantum basis of our DNA, or our Quantum Consciousness."* *(P. Garyaev)* The use of the correct language in self-expression is the pivotal thing because *"human mind and the Mind of the Universe are of the quantum nature.( (Quantum Mind Theory, Hameroff and Penrose A* thoughtless, incorrect language use damages our DNA, and it negatively affects our intellectually spiritualized self-growth. **LANGAUGE CONSCIOUSNESS** is our basic one!

So, we should use robot-humanoids to teach us to become *language-controlled to be exact thinking* in the battle for our priority and human exceptionality. Digital intelligence is damaging our <u>language -consciousness</u> if there is no awareness of the necessity to raise it with constant and conscious self-control of the *language habits and speech skills. (See "Language Intelligence or Universal English."* <u>To succeed, be language -fit!</u>

### "Dissipated consciousness is a wasted life."*( Carl Yung)*

Thus, in our quest for the meaning of the new **CONCEPTUAL STRUCTURE** of life, we will be learning <u>to mentor and monitor ourselves.</u> We desperately need to develop these qualities because our evolutionary goal is to *obtain the ability to decipher the meanings of the universal digital text* that is sent to every cell in our bodies. It puts us into <u>a fractal unity.</u>

### ( Body+ Spirit+ Mind + Self-Consciousness + Super-Consciousness)

## <u>Generalize – Internalize - Personalize – Strategize - Actualize!</u>

## Trans-Human Creation is in our New Fractal Formation!

## Develop Your Vision with Spiritual Provision!

*( Best Pictures, Internet Collection)*

## Faith Decides Timing of Your Self-Rising and Self-Redefining!

## Spiritual Exceptionality

*Self-Ignition Zone*

# God and Me

# are

# In Unity!

*"Look for God in Yourself. "*

*( Prophet Muhammad)*

**"Any Sufficiently Advanced Technology is Indistinguishable from Divinity"**

*( Arthur C. Clarke )*

# 1. Self-Elevation is a Must for Self-Salvation!

Spirituality is the zone of conscience and intuition. <u>God provides our spiritual nutrition!</u> We talk a lot about spirituality and consciousness, but we hardly ever mention <u>the rotting of our conscience</u> and its social pollution in us now, at the time of the digital expansion and mass media electronic indoctrination. *Honor, nobility, and sincerity have become anachronisms* that we need to revive to survive. *Schopenhauer* wrote, defining conscience,

## "Honor is inner conscience, and conscience is inner honor."

*Conscience and intuition are our direct lines to the Super-Consciousness* that we perceive as God. The ancient wisdom says that you can sleep tight if your conscience is clean. It is so true because *it is our conscience that makes us feel inner discomfort* if we said or did something despicable, under the influence of our impulsive behavior patterns and emotions of fear, anger, and self-discontent. Imperfections should first be consciously reasoned out and then consistently tamed!*( See Dr. Joe Dispenza's talks on YouTube)*

### To self-refine, we must be spiritually soul-divine!

*Pricks of conscienc*e are very painful to experience, and the people of all faiths feel them, irrespective of any dogmas or interpretations. In his wonderful story " *"Man is Alive not by Bread Alone, "Leo Tolstoy* writes about the importance of listening to your own conscience in any religion. "*Christ is a great teacher. He preached the common religion of "love for thy neighbor." But God had also other followers, and it does not lower the uniqueness of Christ, it just is the acknowledgement of the greatness of God." Jalaluddin Rumi wrote,*

### "True faith is to learn to please God."

<u>Spiritual exceptionality</u> is, therefore, the ability to respect faith in all its forms and live by its values" <u>to please God.</u>" *Nikola Tesla* believed in the Universal Intelligence that governed all his discoveries. He said in one of his interviews, "*There is a certain core in space. We get our knowledge from it."* Speaking about human capabilities, he added

### " It is wrong to say that a man cannot jump over his head. A man can do anything!"

In sum, conscience, and intuition, as well as our sincere following the provisions of faith help <u>us exercise a strong moral character</u> without which exceptionality will never surface. I am sure the machine-mind should also be intuitively kind! Can we program the humanoids for such fragilities of feelings in their mechanical dealing? I am sure robot humanoids should be programmed in five realms of life, too.

## "No Society Can Develop without a Religious Discipline."

*(Nikola Tesla )*

## 2. Clean Your Inner Digitized Space with Grace!

*Try to live spiritually,*

*And not take your problems virtually*

*For, "As it is Above,*

*So, it is below!"*

*That's where we should go*

*When we feel blue or low!*

*I am strong in my above ways,*

*But I am weak in my personal surveys.*

*So now, when life goes off the normal tract,*

*I don't declare this negative fact.*

*I try to ignore it and disregard,*

*And I am quite good at that!*

*I am happy, anyway,*

*With every passing day!*

*And my new spiritual path*

*Has nothing to do with any depressive mass.*

*So, when asked, "Are you happy, or what?"*

*I give a straightforward "Yes" retort!*

*I am happy that I am alive,*

*Healthy, beautiful, and in love with life!*

*I am also in love with love*

*For everything below and above!*

*Love is my life's load,*

*It's my spiritual code!*

*Changing my emotional plane,*

*I shape myself spiritually again and again!*

*Thus, the inner dignity of the whole*

*Forms the aristocratism of my soul!*

----------------------------

## Life Has Sense Only When It has a High Intellectually Spiritualized Motive!

### The Fractal of Intellectually Spiritualized Being:

*Form*      +      *Content*

(Body+ Spirit+ Mind) + (Self-Consciousness + Universal Consciousness)

*Living Intelligence* + *Enlightened Self-Consciousness* = *A Whole Self!*

----------------------------

*"Let your light so shine before men that they may see your good works."* (Jesus Christ)"

*"God is a supercomputer mind that contains a total inventory of what each of us is."*

(Rev. P. S. Berg /"Taming the Chaos")

*"In the soul, every man is a God or a devil, a hero, or a villain. The proportion is determined by his heart and the mind."*

(Feodor Dostoevsky/ "Brothers Karamazov")

----------------------------

## "Everything We Manage to Accomplish is Left for People, Coming after Us!"

*Leo Tolstoy / "What a Man Lives by."*

# 3. Accumulate Spiritual Exceptionality without any Religious Vanity!

**In sum**, I am sure you have met people who have *personal integrity and strong inner magnetism*. And they are not necessarily priests, prophets, monks, or gurus. Such people have a lot of openness, sincerity of belief, wisdom, and a lot of charisma. We respectfully call them spiritually accomplished, but their accomplishments are not measured by their bank accounts, career positions, and impressive possessions.

**They are self-educated, holistically developed Self-Tamed people.**

The spiritual side of their personalities is rich, and it is always *mind and heart catching.* The pyramid of their intellectualized spirituality is complete.

## They are Self-Installed in God!

There is also a lot of *spiritualized intelligence* in them, respectful **EMOTIONAL DIPLOMACY**, and exceptionally insightful psychological and cultural awareness. Their exceptionality is very modest; there is no arrogance or blind self-confidence in them. They do not sound or look fake. When people of a double-faced spiritual value try to preach what they do not practice themselves, they are straightforward, honest, and objective. They know the value of their own mind. **They are soul-refined!**

**They practice what they preach , and that is why they are exceptional!**

The five-dimensional pyramid of self-development is mastered by them at all the levels, not just a physical one, and it is never supplemented with a declarative exclusion of other faiths. **They have inclusive hearts and minds of exceptional kinds!** The people of spiritual exceptionality demonstrate self-monitoring in the spiritual and soul-refining sense.

In contrast, there are many people who might look successful outwardly, but they are normally very emotionally and psychologically messed up inwardly because *their faith is not exceptional in its depth*. **It is often money-chasing and self-vanity glazing!** Such people do not attend intellectual talks and life-defining meetings with great authors, philosophers, and scientists. **To be in the informational flow, be aware of what you do not know!**

Obviously, spiritual exceptionality cannot be realized without a substantial human effort that should sound in synch with the sacred geometry of the Universe that *"rings as a bell." ( Nikola Tesla)* We can make life beautiful or ugly. If we do it consciously, it will be beautiful, if we do it compulsively, it will be ugly. The AI developers must be exceptional in this way.

# To Life-Rein, New Neural Pathways Must be Established in the Brain!

# The Level of Our Luminosity is Now in Virtual Velocity!

**The Universal Wires of Information Constitute Our Digitized Elation!**

## Universal Exceptionality

*Self-Gravity Zone*

# The Cradle of Humanity is Rocked by the Cosmic Vanity!

*"Creation of the Visible from the Invisible Creates the World!"* ( *Nikola Tesla* )

**To Be Universally "Wired", We Need to Be Beauty of Life and Love Inspired!**

# 1. Live in Sync with the Universal Information Link!

Your exceptionality at the Universal realm of self-growth means *you are in rhythm with Super-Consciousness in the physical, emotional, mental, spiritual, and universal strata of life*. **You are whole, you are alive!**

There are many wise people on Earth who have earned *the state of Salvation* thanks to their godliness, inner luminosity, good deeds, and love that they are able to radiate with their thinking, speaking, feeling, acting, and Universal life perceiving. We call them scientists, prophets, saints, gurus, luminaries, and chanteclers. *They live by the Universal Laws, and they never betray them.*

## "As it is Above, so, it is below" That's how they go!

Unfortunately, the information that YouTube channels provide swirls our brains into *an informational turmoil* that needs a lot of scanning for its validity, *on the one hand*, and a lot of cleaning and systematizing of the information *on the other*. The mess of the information unconsciously perceived and processed in a superficial way does not give us the chance **to single out the grains of wisdom** that the most exceptional people communicate to us

It is a pity *we get these pearls of knowledge* among the cooking lessons, hints on make-up usage, sleazy stories about celebrities, and other *"news salads"* and different *"cookies,"* meant to sweeten the appalling general ignorance of the public. But if you are seriously on the path of *Self-Resurrection*, **you should be the one responsible for the mental food that you digest**! It is less time-consuming and very rewarding to follow *your own mental diet.*

Upload the information that fits your self-growth interests, *depositing it into the brain compartments*, suitable for this information and consciously link it to the information deposits that you have already made before.

*Being whole also means having the brain holistically connected to the mind!*

*Have a special notebook for your own important news.* Divide the list into two parts. Devote the *left-brain section* for the bits of news, quotes, ideas etc. that you paid aware attention to. *The right-brain part* of the list should be devoted to *your opinion on this information*, your agreement, disagreement, new creative ideas, etc. I have collected such notebooks since 1994, and these notebooks have become my " food for thought" for all my 24 published books.

# Self-Synthesis – Self-Analysis – Self-Synthesis!

## 2. Let's Raise Our Boys as Real Men!

*(An Instructional Booster)*

*Let's raise our boys as Real Men!*

*Digitally enlightened in their stem!*

*A real man is not a cloud in the pants,*

*He's the one with the iron-clad guts!*

---------------------------

*In his mental fest,*

*He can conquer Everest!*

*And in his emotional out-let,*

*He needs to be a real athlete,*

*Able to feel, to support, to kneel,*

*And to sustain a marriage deal.*

*To stand tall and to forestall*

*Any financial downfall!*

*To rise from ashes again and again*

*And to be able to rule the Carforgen!*

---------------------------

*His castle of love*

*Is made of strong stuff!*

*His individual whims,*

*Regrets, doubts, and money spins*

*Should not bother him a bit*

*If he wants to fit*

*A rare uniform*

*For the best human form!*

-----------------------

*I wish every woman, at that*

*To find a man like that!*

*For the more intelligent is the man,*

*The better woman you can become!*

*This formula works the other way, too,*

*If a man wants to become a success guru!*

*Behind a man's uplifted thumb*

*Is the love and support of his damme !*

--------------------------

*So, let's raise our boys as real men,*

*Able to strengthen the human stem!*

*For Real Men*

*Are the co-creators of the Universal Eden!*

----------------------------

**Theirs is the Future. It is Mutual!**


**Long Live the Belief in Our Kids without "IF!"**

# 3. The Triumph of the Spirit over the Body is Our Universal Glory!

**In sum**, you need to constantly reflect on your inner technologically expanding range **in the vectors of time** (*the vertical arrow*), indicating **mind** evolution and **in the vector of space** (*the horizontal arrow*), signifying **body** evolution in time and space. The zero position of this matrix indicates **the spirit** that must always be the gluing element **in the intellectually spiritualized fractal of self-growth that was universally reflected in such people as:** *Albert Einstein, Nikola Tesla, and Steve Jobs.* It has its reflection on our great contemporaries – the most exceptional scientists, AI developers, engineers and just very hard-working people that make the present-day wonders possible. Led by the strategically thinking minds of ***Bill Gates, Elon Musk, Jeff Bezos, Mark Zuckerberg, David Hanson, and the other most amazing creators of robot-humanoids.***

No doubt, Inspiration, incredible dedication to an exceptional goal , and positive self-boosting are pivotal for the objective work on the preservation of the health of the mind and its exceptional self-expression. To fortify them, we need to always keep the **form** and the **content** of life coordinated.

**Health, happiness, and success are therefore the result of a conscious internal unifying**!

**(Body+ Spirit+ Mind) + ( Self-Consciousness + Universal Consciousness)**

***Your spirit is also the basis for*** *the mind + heart* ***sync.***

## The Defeat of the Spirit over the Body is your Folly!

## To Self-Excel, never lose your Spirit's Spell!

If you start losing your spirit, you will feel that your *fractal holistic Self* is getting weak and inwardly broken**.** *Immediately boost your spirit with one of the mind-sets,* stored in your memory bank or in a smartphone for such episodes and make yourself **form + content whole** again. At any shaky time, try to get in touch with the most advanced and enlightened people in person or in virtual communication.

You will always demonstrate an *amazing personal integrity, faith, and a strong personality magnetism* that you need to constantly charge. Be sure to illuminate negative people from your virtual space. *Feel free to call me ( 203)212-2673 or email me (* *dr.rimaletta@gmail.com* *) for free advice.*

*It takes only a stroke to change a minus into a plus and build yourself back, thus!*

# Be Part of a New Seeing. You Are a Universal Being!

# I Am in Love with Life, and Life is in Love with Me.

**Our Common Might is in**
**The Eternal Luminosity of Light!**

## Conclusion of the Inspirational Infusion

# Live with Zest.

# Exceptional Life is

# Abreast!

**With a Sincere Zest, you will Win Your Life's Exceptional Quest!**

# 1. Vistas of Conceptual Intelligence

**In conclusion**, let's get back to the cones of the vistas of intelligence , presented as your top mental goal in *the first chunk* of information, illustrating **MENTAL EXCEPTIONALITY**. above. Every level of your *Intellectually Spiritualized Self-Resurrection* brings you up to new digitally enhanced abilities, new revived **LANGAUGE CONSCIOUSNESS** and **SELF-CONSCIOUSNESS,** forming the indispensable for our time and *Artificial Super Intelligence* enhanced **CONCEPTUAL INTELLIGENCE.**

From the **Micro** level to the **Macro** and **Super** ones, we deal with five **levels of general intelligence** that the process of self-growth perfection is propelling in us through at the AI exceptional times. In fact, we are developing an **INTEGRATED WEB of INTELLIGENCE** based on our electronic language intelligence. Our Conceptual Intelligence *gets integrated into the new, technology-based,* **Integral Social intelligence**, based on the ten basic vistas of Intelligence , essential for our conceptual vision of the world at the time of AI expansion.

### The Levels of Conceptual Intelligence Formation

| | | |
|---|---|---|
| **Super Level** *(Language Mastery)* | | *Social Intelligence* |
| **Macro Level** *(Language Utilization)* | | *Cultural Intelligence* |
| **Mezzo Level** *(Language Management)* | | *Professional Intelligence* |
| **Meta Level** *(Language Actualization)* | | *Emotional Intelligence* |
| **Micro Level** *(Language Creation)* | | *Language Intelligence* |

**Language Intelligence** *(Self-Awareness*) is the basis of your general intelligence that incorporates your language / speech competence and helps you articulate your intelligent needs, be argumentative, think critically, and promote your ideas in the *mind-to-mind and heart-to-heart* digital and *face-to face* .interaction.

**Emotional Intelligence** *(Self-Monitoring )* helps you monitor your feelings by developing Emotional *Diplomacy skills.*

**Professional Intelligence** *(Self-Installation)* is your operational intelligence in life, your professional intelligence. It helps you continuously improve your *Self-Installation skills.*

**Cultural Intelligence** *( Self-Realization)* helps you in a dynamic interchange among cultures, expand your knowledge base in other cultures' art, literature, science to be a well-cultured person that fits perfectly in the fast-changing, *Artificial Intelligence enhanced* world.

**Social Intelligence** *(Self-Salvation) It engages* you in the present-day social networking and takes you to a new level of social interaction in which the role of English is dominant.

*Physical Form* + *Spiritual Content*

**(Body+ Spirit+ Mind) + (Self-Consciousness + Universal Consciousness)**

**= Human Exceptionality of Spiritual Adulthood.**

# Fractal Formation is Our Common Universal Donation.

## 2. Check Your Exceptionality in Eveready's Reality!

*Every day, when you are without any mask,*

*You must address yourself and ask,*

*"What have I done today*

*For my physical array?*

*Have I added a bit*

*To my emotional upbeat?*

*Have I enriched*

*My mental outreach?*

*And , finally on the spiritual plane,*

*Have I gotten closer to God's Domain?*

*So, don't waste your daily zest*

*To just possess!*

*Use it to infuse*

*Your self-realization fuse!*

------------

**Reminder:** *get into the habit* **of SCANNING YOURSELF OBJECTIVELY** *in five dimensions every night before you fall asleep. Do it in most general terms, assessing our actions for* **the physical state, emotional control, mental enrichment, spiritual sustainability, and the dedication to your universally blessed exceptional mission or the goal of life.** *Even if your present-day job or unfavorable circumstances keep you away from it,* **do not betray your exceptionality** *and get closer to its sincere expression and full realization every day. Give yourself grades for each level and a general grade for the day.* **You are your own Best Friend. You are your Beginning and your End!**

# On the Scales of Your Life's Surf, Stay Balanced and Reserved!

# 3. RULES FOR OUR DIGITALLY ENHANCED INNER JOY TO LIFE-ENJOY!

1.To Be Spiritually Bold, Fit in the New Life's Mold!

2. Put Your Life in Sync with an Unbreakable Form + Content life link! Feel but think!

*Form* + *Content*

(Body + Spirit + Mind) + (Self-Consciousness + Universal Consciousness) =

*Physical. + emotional + .mental + spiritual + universal dimension of life*

-----------------------------

3.*Follow the Holistic Paradigm in your thinking, speaking, feeling, acting, and Self-Refining.*

*Self-Synthesis - Self-Analysis – Self-Synthesis!*

5. *Internalize Your Emotions and Externalize the Mind!*

*Be One of a Kind!*

6. *Kill the doubt in the bud and be very strong at that!*

7. *To have a solid sanity, conquer your personal vanity!*

8. *Be Kind to the Unkind. Be One of a Kind!*

9. *Self-Taming is life-gaining!*

10.*Use digital technology for your Holistic Self-Ecology!*

11. *Consciously infuse your Self-Worth fuse!*

12. *Your main self-exceptionality mind-set is:*

Appreciate Your Uniqueness and Work on the Bleakness!

## Being the Best is a Tough Test!

## 4. To Live with Universal Intelligence in Synch, <u>Create the Mind + Heart Link!</u>

*The mind and heart's link*

*Needs to be always in sync*

*With a person's soul*

*That must be self-consoled!*

*The soul that responds,*

*Vibrates, and resonates*

*To the heart's surcharge*

<u>*Always, not once!*</u>

*The soul that reflects*

*The rays of kindness, passion, and compassion!*

*Then, the Sun's rays*

*Will warm up the soul's space*

*Around a person's Merkabah*

*And delete its evil abracadabra.*

*The core of the Merkabah's link*

*Is in the heart + mind sync!*

*Only this consonance*

*Can fix our outer dissonance!*

----------------------

<u>I know who I am and who I am Not. That's my Spiritual Fort!</u>

## "Life is the Rhythm that You Need to Tune Up to."

*( Nikola Tesla)*

# 5. Inspirational Psychology of Self-Ecology!

Your Self-*Resurrection* must be completed *physically, emotionally, mentally, and universally.*

**Your Trans-Human Creation is in a New Fractal Formation!**

**(Body+ Spirit+ Mind) + (Self-Consciousness + Universal Consciousness)**

**== Human Exceptionality of the Intellectually Spiritualized Adulthood.**

As a holistically integrated human being, you can declare your wholeness to boost your confidence:

**My Heart is Smart, and the Mind is Kind!**

**I Am One of a Kind!**

**I am physically**

**Beautiful.**

**I am emotionally**

**Invincible.**

**I am mentally**

**Unbeatable.**

**I am spiritually**

**Free.**

**And Universally-**

**I Am an Exceptional Me!**

**I generalize, internalize, personalize, strategize, and actualize my Life. I am Consciously Alive!**

**Digitized Self-Acculturation is My Salvation!**

# 6. Attitude of Gratitude

**In sum**, undeniably, we are not perfect yet, but it will gradually happen that we all will become more *humane, positively minded, spiritually whole, and scientifically advanced people of the Earth,* able to **CONQURE** other planets and create life there, making our exceptional mission complete.

### Hurray to all exceptional minds of today!!!

*I would like to favor my wonderful parents, **Sergey and Nina Zhenkov,** Academician **A.A. Leontief**, my scientific mentor, my best American friends, an exceptional businessman **Fred Cronin** and his late wife, **Barbara**, my best African American student that has created himself following my paradigm, **Fran Telima,** the Shop Rite Store manager of rare people-caring skills, **Maggie Leo-Pierre,** and many other, randomly met godly people who have left the marks of wisdom in my soul that inspired me.*

*My deepest attitude of gratitude to **the exceptional minds of all great world scientists** whose ideas have backed up mine and who I have quoted a lot in all my books. All these exceptional people **have framed my personality and their minds have enlightened and enriched mine.***

*Please, **list below the names of the exceptional people** that have impacted your self-growth and that you favor most for their contribution to your life.*

-------------------------------------------------------------

### Being Grateful makes us Exceptional and Never Forgetful!

There will still be many evil-minded people among us, but their number will be considerably diminished with our common effort *to better our humaneness* to deserve admission to the *Star Community*, explore life beyond the terrestrial boundaries, and install the best qualities of **heart + mind** connection in ourselves and in our kids.

Developing our own self-exceptionality, we are generating *Universal Love* and *Harmony* in the hearts and minds of our kids and grandkids that would do the impossible after us in the vast cosmic plane of *the multi verse domain.*

## I Wish I Could Live then in the Unanswerable WHEN!

## Universal Mind of the Sun!

# 7. Our Salvation is in Self-Acculturation!

"We Think that We are Born into the World, but the Truth is the World is Born into You!"

*"In the end,
only three things matter:
how much you loved,
how gratefully you lived,
and how gracefully
you let go of things
not meant for you."*

(Buddha)

**Digital Phycology + Self-Ecology + Language Purity =**

**SELF-ACCULTURATION**

# Turn on The Sun of Your Soul and Be Exceptionally Whole!

**I Never Whine; I Just Shine!**

## 8. To Conclude, I am Passing over My Favorite Self-Induction to Thee:

# Appreciate Your Life in its Entire Mass for It Too Shall Pass!

**Always Tune Your Love to the Station Above!**

# Dr. Ray with her Inspirational Say!

## Books on Language Intelligence:

*1. "Language Intelligence or Universal English"* (Method of the Right Language Behavior), **Book One** /Xlibris, 2013

*2. "Language Intelligence or Universal English"* (Remedy Your Language Habits," **Book Two** /Xlibris, 2013–

*3. "Language Intelligence or Universal English,"* (Remedy Your Speech Skills) **Book Three** /Xlibris, 2013

*4. " Language Intelligence or Universal English!( republished in one book , Stone Wall Press, USA / 2019*

**5.**.*"Americanize Your Language, Emotionalize Your Speech!"* / Nova Press, USA, 2011

### Books on Inspirational Psychology for Self-Ecology:

*6. "**Emotional Diplomacy** or **Follow the Bliss of the Uncatchable Is!**"/ **Editorial** LEIRIS, New York, USA,2005, 2010*

*7.***"Five Dimensions of the Soul***" / in Russian, LEIRIS Publishing, New York, USA, 2011*

*8.***"It Too Shall Pass!"** (Inspirational Boosters in Five Dimensions) / Xlibris, 2012*

*Second Edition – by Workbook Press -2020*

*9.***"I am Strong in My Spirit!"** (Inspirational Boosters in Russian) / Xlibris, 2013**.**

*10..***"My Solar System,"** (Auto-Suggestive Psychology for Inner Ecology) Xlibris, 2015 republished*

*11.***Second Edition by UR Link Print and Media, 2020**

### Books on Self-Resurrection in five life dimensions:

*(Physical, emotional, mental, spiritual, universal )*

*12.***"I Am Free to Be the Best of Me!"**- ( **Physical Dimension**) - Toplinkpublishing.com. Sept. 2017) – Second Edition , Book Whip, 2019- **Second Edition***

*13..* **Soul-Refining!** (**Emotional Dimension**) (Toplinkpublishing.com. May 2017) - **Second Edition by Global Summit House, 2020**

14. *"Living Intelligence or the Art of Becoming!"* ( *Mental Dimension*)- *Xlibris, 2015 – Second Edition (Bookwhip, 2019-***Third Edition- by Global Summit House, 2020 / Excellence Book Award, 2020**

15. *"Self-Taming"* ( *Life-Gaining is in Self-Taming!)( Spiritual Dimension)-* Book Whip, 2019- **Second Edition by Global Summit House, 2020**

16. .*" Beyond the Terrestrial!"* (Be the Station for Self-Inspiration*!) - (Universal Dimension ) /-* First Edition-Xlibris, 2016*./ .* **Second Edition** */* Book Whip, 2018   **7. Third Edition** – UR Link Print and Media, 2019

17..*'" The State of Love from the Above!"- Book Whip, 2018  / "Love Ecology"- Dr. Rimaletta Ray Publishing.,* New Jersey,  **2020**

18. **" Love Ecology"( Love is Me; Love is My Philosophy!)**

19. *"Self-Worth "- Parchment Publishing ,  New York , 2020*

20. **"Self- Renaissance"** *– Workbook , Las Vegas, 2021*

### Book on  Digital Psychology for Self-Ecology

21.  **"Soul-Symmetry!", Canadoa,2021**

22. **"Dis-Entangle-ment!"-** *Ivy Lit Press, New York ,2022*

23. **"Digital Binary + Human Refinery=Super-Human!"** */ Stellar Literary, 2023 )*

## Self-Acculturation is Our Salvation!

*www. Language – fitness.com / Trailer - Section "Self-Resurrection"*

*See  seven videos on YouTube / Dr. Rimaletta Ray and "Dis-Entanglement "*

*email  - dr.rimaletta@gmail.com*

**Tel. (203) 212-26734**

# Live with a Zest.
# Exceptional Life is Abreast!